ELEMENTS OF GRACE

BARKLEY S. THOMPSON

TRINITY BOOKS

ELEMENTS OF GRACE

ISBN: 978-0615923901

TRINITY BOOKS
an imprint of The Global Gospel, LLC
184 N. George Circle
Marion, Arkansas 72364

"If I say, 'I will not mention him, or speak any more in his name',
then within me there is something like a burning fire shut up in my bones;
I am weary with holding it in, and I cannot."

Jeremiah 20:9

For Jill, Griffin, and Eliza

Table of Contents

Foreword

One morning on my way into work I heard a wonderful meditation on the "last survivors." I heard it on a radio program called *Engines of Our Ingenuity*. The program's long-time host talked about the last person who knew Vincent Van Gogh, the last survivor of Custer's battle at Little Big Horn, the last survivor of the Civil War, and the last Civil War veteran's widow, who died in 2003.[1] I was struck by how our lives overlap and how events and stories are carried through time by real people in real relationships.

I wondered whose lifetimes had crossed my own. In almost five decades there were many.

Ruth Dyk, died November 18, 2000 (age 99), last suffragette

Dimitrios Loundras, died February 15, 1971 (age 84), last known living competitor at the 1896 Summer Olympics

Aurelio Diaz Campillo, died June 13, 1989 (age 110), last Spanish veteran of the Spanish-American War

Maude Conic, died November 14, 2004 (age 106), last survivor of the Galveston Hurricane of 1900

Alexander Bernard Heron, died January 24, 2000 (age 105), last worker involved in the construction of the Panama Canal

Frank Buckles, died February 27, 2011 (age 110), last American veteran of World War I

James Cameron, died June 11, 2006 (age 92), last individual to survive a lynching attempt in the U.S.

Miep Gies, died January 11, 2010 (age 100), last member of the "Secret Annex" that hid Anne Frank during WWII

Harold Stassen, died March 4, 2001 (age 93), last signer of the United Nations Charter

Arieh Handler, died May 20, 2011 (age 95), last witness to the signing of the Israeli Declaration of Independence

Zelma Henderson, died May 20, 2008 (age 88), last participant in the *Brown v. Board of Education* case

There are, of course, many, many more. Yet these somehow touch the events and lives lived in my time. They are the backstory to events that continue to affect the world in which we live. Some are people of whom I have never heard. Lives lived and events witnessed. They were part of history. Their faith, their own life narrative, their own view of history affected many untold thousands of people as did the events to which their names are attached.

The letter of Hebrews reminds us that we are connected. We are connected to people who long ago had faith and navigated their world based upon their faith. Some had great faith, some had complex faith, and some had simple faith. We are changed as a result of how they lived their faith.

The author of Hebrews reminds us of Enoch, who pleased God in his lifetime by believing and doing good works. He reminds us of Abel, whose faith led him to give thanks to God. There is Abraham who had faith, listened to God and followed. There are Isaac and Jacob, who built up the family of God and gathered around them a great host of believers and brought about a city of God—and Sarah, whose faith led to the building of a nation of people. The author reminds us that from creation, to the Red Sea, and to the walls of Jerusalem, people have been responding to faith in a God who has made all things.

"And what more should I say?" Hebrews tells us. "For time would fail me to tell of Gideon, Barak, Samson, Jephthah, of David and Samuel and the prophets—who through faith conquered kingdoms, administered justice, obtained promises, shut the mouths of lions, quenched raging fire, escaped the edge of the sword, won strength out of weakness, became mighty in war, put foreign armies to flight ... They wandered in deserts and mountains, and in caves and holes in the ground. Yet all these, though they were commended for their faith, did not receive what was promised, since God had provided something better so that they would not, apart from us, be made perfect."[2]

These are not stories to remind us of great men and women who lived some time long ago—in an age of heroes and kings. They are offered to us so that we may see regular people living regular lives. The list of survivors and the list of biblical names offer to us the notion that we, in our lives, are the saints of this age. We are the sinners becoming saints, who are navigating a new age and telling and retelling the story of faith to those around us. We are making our faithful response. They were known in their day as God's people by their faith; so shall we be known. No matter how hard or difficult life was or how long and arduous the journey, they followed and they shaped history around them.

The life of faith, the creative vibrant life of faith, is always lived in response to God and to Jesus. This is our privilege, this is our calling, this is what we do as Christians. In fact, as faithful people—not unlike the gathering cloud of witnesses—it is our heart's song to live in response to this God who beckons us into a mission of love and to embrace our neighbor.

The God they believed in could not be touched. This God is a surprising God, appearing in fire and darkness, in tempests and on mountains. This God is a God whose presence shakes the earth, and who moves across the waters like a hovering wind. This God is a God unlike us, yet a God who longs to be with us. This God walks in the garden in the cool of the evening, leads his people with a fiery pillar, and appears in human form to the poor and the weak. The God they believed in and that we believe in still is a wild God. Our God is a God of the wild places and of wild people. Our God is in the midst of the world and brings creativity where there is need of it and chaos where there is need of it.

We reside in this God's kingdom. It is this God whom we follow—the God who shakes our foundations and offers us abundant life in a realm that cannot be shaken. It is this God that we worship and to whom we offer our lives and ministry. It is this God who consumes us in his love. It is this God who sets our hearts on fire because of his love. Our God is a God of terrifying, quickening and gentle love.

Paul Tillich wrote a wonderful book entitled *The Shaking of the Foundations*, which I have often enjoyed. In the opening chapter, Tillich writes:

> *How could the prophets speak as they did? How could they paint these most terrible pictures of doom and destruction without cynicism or despair? It was because, beyond the sphere of destruction, they saw the sphere of salvation; because in the doom of the temporal, they saw the manifestation of the Eternal. It was because they were certain that they belonged within the two spheres, the changeable and the unchangeable. For only he who is also beyond the changeable, not bound within it alone, can face the end. All others are compelled to escape, to turn away ... For in these days the foundations of the earth do shake. May we not turn our eyes away; rather see, through the crumbling of a world, the rock of eternity and the salvation which has no end!*[B]

Elements of Grace by The Very Rev. Barkley Thompson is about the interconnectedness of our stories. It is about the connection of lives lived today with the living Word of Scripture and the lives within. It is about the lives of saints and sinners from times past and times present and the discovery that we are family. It is about a God of the wild places who interacts in the midst of human lives. It is about a God who reaches out to us and loves us. It is about a God who shakes the foundations of the world, the powers that be, and our lives and offers unshakeable hope in the future.

It is a timely offering as the world continues to move into the new millennium in which we are called to make our witness. In the pages that follow we find we are not alone in our pilgrimage to God. Herein we discover we are not orphans, but we are brothers and sisters in a great migration, making its way into the kingdom of God. We discover that our lives matter and have the possibility of making a difference in the world around us and in the lives connected with our own.

We are surrounded by a great a cloud of witnesses, so let us lay down the burden that clings so closely to us and pulls us back. Let us run with perseverance and resolve the race that is before us in our time and in our context. Let us read in these pages a sure and certain hope that Jesus walks before us. And, as we make our way in the fog of the stresses and strains of life today, Jesus even in this hour beckons us follow.[4]

The Right Reverend C. Andrew Doyle
IX Bishop of Texas
The Episcopal Church

ENDNOTES

1 John Lienhard, "Last Survivors," Episode 2187 of *Engines of Our Ingenuity* radio broadcast, available online at http://www.uh.edu/engines/epi2187.htm (accessed October 25, 2013).

2 Hebrews 11:29ff. (NRSV).

3 Paul Tillich, *The Shaking of the Foundations* (New York: Charles Scribner's Sons, 1953), 11.

4 Hebrews, 12:1ff (NRSV).

Preface

"Taking once again a fresh starting point suitable to the matter…we must gain a view of the real nature of fire and water, air and earth, as it was before the birth of Heaven, and the properties they had before that time…and we call them principles and presume that they are elements of the Universe."

Plato, Timaeus, 48b[1]

"In the beginning when God created the heavens and the earth, the earth was a formless void and darkness covered the face of the deep, while a spirit from God swept over the face of the waters. Then God said, 'Let there be light'; and there was light. And God saw that the light was good; and God separated the light from the darkness."

Genesis 1:1-4

In classical thought, the four elements were the basic and essential building blocks of reality, with which all else was constructed and through which all was experienced. For the ancients, the elements most often named were earth, air, fire and water. Sometimes a fifth, the aether, was included.

Theologically and with a bit of adaptation, this idea retains its potency. There are, indeed, basic and essential elements through which we encounter God and experience the grace of the Gospel, articulated in the first four verses of Holy Scripture: *Earth, water, spirit* (from the Hebrew *ruach*, which also refers to air, breath), *light,* and *darkness.* Darkness, as the absence of light, is admittedly not an element in the proper sense. And yet, particularly (and perhaps paradoxically) on Ash Wednesday, Good Friday, and occasions of anguish or grief, it is in the inky and unrelenting darkness that we cleave to God.

To these five we must add *discipleship,* which is the elementary function of those who claim Jesus Christ as Lord. Finally—but only in the sense that the last shall be first—there is the *Word,* the element essential even to the other elements, through whom all things come into being and without whom not one thing comes into being (John 1:3).

I have discovered that my preaching unwittingly gravitates to these elements of grace, and consequently arranging this compilation of sermons according to such a schema, rather than by the seasons of the liturgical year or some other arrangement, made immediate and obvious sense.

These sermons were preached over the course of a decade, mostly from the pulpits of the Church of the Holy Apostles in Collierville, Tennessee and St. John's Church in Roanoke, Virginia. A few were delivered while I served as guest preacher at events in other churches and cities. They are, as are all sermons I preach, specifically contextual. Even so, I hope for the reader the context informs and illumines rather than impedes the sermon.

Among the vast Communion of Saints to whom I extend my appreciation, I must mention several by name. Thanks to Nelda Horton and Anne Shepherd for their efforts to bring my idiosyncratic footnotes into conformity with Kate Turabian. Thanks also to Andrew Thompson and Matt Washburn at Trinity Books for inviting me to publish. I am an Episcopal priest who blessedly was taught to preach by a Baptist, and I am grateful for the wisdom and instruction of the Rev. Roger Paynter. Along with Roger, seminary professors Cynthia Kittredge, Michael Floyd, and Alan Gregory were particularly important to my formation as priest and preacher. For the past thirteen years I have kept close company with four seminary classmates and colleagues without whose friendship and counsel I would be a sorry priest. My gratitude for the lives and ministries of the Revs. Morgan Allen, Daryl Hay, Austin Rios, and Mary Vano knows no bounds. I am thankful for the people of Holy Apostles and St. John's, as well as for the parishioners of Christ Church Cathedral where I presently serve. These congregations inspire my preaching, and it is an honor to walk as a fellow traveler on the Way with such good and faithful people. Finally, I thank God each day for Jill, Griffin and Eliza. Their love sustains me, as I hope mine does them.

ENDNOTES

1 Plato, Timaeus, 48b, in vol. 9 of *Plato in Twelve Volumes*, trans. W.R.M. Lamb (Cambridge, MA: Harvard University Press; London: William Heinemann Ltd., 1925), from the Perseus Digital Library at Tufts University.

Earth

Patches Over Potholes

DECEMBER 2007   MATTHEW 3:1-12

"In those days John the Baptist appeared in the wilderness of Judea, proclaiming, "Repent, for the kingdom of heaven has come near." This is the one of whom the prophet Isaiah spoke when he said, "The voice of one crying out in the wilderness: 'Prepare the way of the Lord, make his paths straight.'" Now John wore clothing of camel's hair with a leather belt around his waist, and his food was locusts and wild honey. Then the people of Jerusalem and all Judea were going out to him, and all the region along the Jordan, and they were baptized by him in the river Jordan, confessing their sins.

But when he saw many Pharisees and Sadducees coming for baptism, he said to them, "You brood of vipers! Who warned you to flee from the wrath to come? Bear fruit worthy of repentance. Do not presume to say to yourselves, 'We have Abraham as our ancestor'; for I tell you, God is able from these stones to raise up children to Abraham. Even now the ax is lying at the root of the trees; every tree therefore that does not bear good fruit is cut down and thrown into the fire. "I baptize you with water for repentance, but one who is more powerful than I is coming after me; I am not worthy to carry his sandals. He will baptize you with the Holy Spirit and fire. His winnowing fork is in his hand, and he will clear his threshing floor and will gather his wheat into the granary; but the chaff he will burn with unquenchable fire."

"It will build character," he said, as if that were some solace to a nineteen-year-old. I had come home from my freshman year at college, and my father had insisted that I take a job doing manual labor. He had worked on the railroad during the summers of his youth to help put food on the table, and he wanted a similar experience for his own boys.

I knew when arguing with my Dad might get me somewhere—which is to say never—and so I signed on with the district bridge crew of the Arkansas Highway Department. Early one July morning we set out to work on a bridge outside the tiny town of Alicia. This was bleak Arkansas wilderness, let me tell you. At first I feared that vultures were flying overhead, but then I realized they were only mosquitoes the size of vultures, ready to carry off small dogs.

We stopped on a county highway bridge over a creek. In the July heat, part of the concrete bridge bed had blown out, or so we thought, and we were to repair it. I soon found myself jackhammering away. I'd learned that the easiest (though surely not safest) way to jackhammer was to lean one's chest on the back of one's hands and press down on the hammer with full weight. That I did, and after a few seconds of jarring vibrations, I felt an odd sensation. Suddenly, all resistance to the hammer was gone, and I realized I was dropping. Somehow I pushed the hammer away from me and then fell backwards. When I stood up I realized what had happened. The pothole in the bridge had not been a hot weather blow out. This bridge was so old and neglected that the concrete bed was rotten. Where I'd been hammering was now a hole all the way to the creek below. The jackhammer and I had almost dropped straight through it.

Our crew chief, Kyle, inspected the situation. He looked through the hole with a rub of his chin and said, "This bridge is rotten." He then instructed two of the guys to drive back to the county yard and pick up several old stop signs. At first I thought Kyle was going to set up warnings at either end of the bridge. Instead, he took those old signs and laid them in the bridge bed to cover up the hole. Then he poured quick-set concrete on top of them, and by the end of the day looked up proudly and said, "Taken care of! No one will know the difference."

Maybe not. It was county highway with little traffic. That make-shift patch might have held up for several years. But the fact remained that the bridge bed was pocked and rotten. It was crooked and bent. It was a highway disaster waiting to happen. And Kyle thought he could remedy it with a quick patch.

I thought of this experience as I studied the Gospel text for today, as it says, "The voice of one crying out in the wilderness: 'Prepare the way [which means the highway, the road] of the Lord, make his paths straight.'"

We immediately assume that the Gospel is referring to John the Baptist as the one crying from the wilderness. After all, John is described to us as one who lives away from society, dressing in animal hide and eating locusts and honey. While others live in civilization, John lives in the wilderness, set apart from the world.

But punctuation in scripture—where to put commas and quotation marks—is a scholarly guess at best. And so, "The voice of one crying out in the wilderness: 'Prepare the highway of the Lord,'" can also equally be read, "The voice of one crying out: '*In the wilderness*, prepare the highway of the Lord.'" Indeed, this is the way it appears in Isaiah, from which the Gospel quotes.

Do you catch the difference? Is it important? Absolutely! Read this second way it is not John—the one crying out—who lives in the wilderness. It is the audience! The wilderness is where those to whom John is speaking find themselves. The saying is, "In the wilderness—in your wilderness—prepare the way of the Lord." The wilderness is not, then, a physical location, but rather the quality of their lives, and the highways they are to prepare are the highways to their hearts along which God will travel to meet each of them.

Were we John's audience, we might take offense at this suggestion. They most likely believe that their lives are healthy and lush with faith and fervor. How dare John suggest that they live in the wilderness! Oh sure, they recognize that there are things in their lives that need mending: a misstep here or a sin there. That's why they are so glad that John is down at the Jordan offering baptism. Baptism, they think, is like a nice patch over the potholes in their lives. They can go and dip in the water and be forgiven.

That's surely what the Sadducees and Pharisees have in mind, but they misunderstand entirely. You see, John doesn't preach patches over potholes. John preaches repentance. Often we think of repentance as a patch—saying "I'm sorry" for something we've done—but such an understanding does not square with the biblical idea of repentance. The word in Greek is *metanoia*, from the same root from which we derive our English word "metamorphosis." It means nothing less than transformation as stark and great as when a caterpillar morphs into a butterfly. *Metanoia*—repentance—is a complete upending of one's life. It's a reorientation of priorities. John message is, "Repent! Prepare the highway of the Lord," and to return to the image of the highway, rather than filling in potholes, repentance is a stripping of the entire roadbed of our lives, replacing the old foundation with one completely new, one that is cemented firmly in the love of God.

The Sadducees and Pharisees have no intention of such a transformation of life. Like my crew chief at the highway department out in the barren wilderness of Northeast Arkansas, they know that in the wilderness of their own inner lives something is rotten, but they think if they patch it over they, too, can say, "Taken care of! No one will know the difference."

But God knows. The Jesus who will come at Christmas knows. And so, we must ask ourselves with discerning hearts and open eyes: Do the highways of our lives travel through the wilderness? Are our roads crooked and bent, leading us in circles back to our own personal, self-serving motives and desires rather than toward a closer, more open relationship with God? Do our lives often seem arid and sparse like the wilderness, with nothing for miles around that moves us to be different, better, and good?

I really wish I could have been at the bank of the Jordan to see how people reacted to John. Many, I'm sure, decided he was crazy. They likely threw back their shoulders and huffed indignantly at his talk. They walked away into their old lives, preferring the patch on the pothole instead of a whole new road.

What they didn't realize, is that in walking away they walked right back into the wilderness. Because the Lord did come. He came to be baptized by John in that same river. They may have walked right passed him! But because the road to their hearts was so crumbled and bent, they did not know him.

Others, though, understood John's call to repent. They left the highways they'd traveled in life and turned toward the Jordan never looking back. They left the wilderness, and when Jesus emerged along the highway they ran to him, sure-footed on the smooth pavement. His love was like an oasis—the very opposite of the wilderness—and in it their lives were transformed.

In just a few weeks time, Advent gives way to the Nativity. Jesus is coming. Are we ready to meet him and be transformed, to give our lives a renewed foundation? On Christmas morning, when the sun rises and the air is crisp, will our first thoughts be of the God who has again been born among us? Will the first tinge in our hearts be of his love? Will our first impulse be how to take to new highways and share this Good News with an aching world, a world that lives in the wilderness?

"Repent," John says, "For the kingdom of heaven is near. In the wilderness, prepare the way of the Lord. Make his path straight." For he is coming. He is coming!

Amen.

The Cloud on the Mountain

AUGUST 2011   MATTHEW 17:1-9

Six days later, Jesus took with him Peter and James and his brother John and led them up a high mountain, by themselves. And he was transfigured before them, and his face shone like the sun, and his clothes became dazzling white. Suddenly there appeared to them Moses and Elijah, talking with him. Then Peter said to Jesus, 'Lord, it is good for us to be here; if you wish, I will make three dwellings here, one for you, one for Moses, and one for Elijah.' While he was still speaking, suddenly a bright cloud overshadowed them, and from the cloud a voice said, 'This is my Son, the Beloved; with him I am well pleased; listen to him!' When the disciples heard this, they fell to the ground and were overcome by fear. But Jesus came and touched them, saying, 'Get up and do not be afraid.' And when they looked up, they saw no one except Jesus himself alone.

As they were coming down the mountain, Jesus ordered them, 'Tell no one about the vision until after the Son of Man has been raised from the dead.'

Since Sir Edmund Hillary first topped Mount Everest, roughly two thousand individuals have made the trek. Everest, more than any other peak, is inherently unpredictable. Atmospheric conditions on the mountain can suddenly shift. The weather can change without a moment's notice. The wind can whip up and clouds can settle, blinding climbers and causing disorientation and desperate confusion. Two thousand individuals have reached Everest's summit, but two hundred—that's ten percent—have died trying. Most often, as I understand it, these are those who, when the air becomes thin, the cloud settles, and their expectations are upended, begin to act erratically and scurry around taking action for action's sake.

Today's Gospel includes mountain climbing. Jesus takes Peter, James, and John up the mountain with him. It is a high mountain, we are told. The four make their climb, and once at the summit Jesus is transformed before the disciples' eyes. His clothes become dazzling white, and alongside him appear Moses and Elijah. In other words, on this mountain for the disciples atmospheric conditions have suddenly shifted! And Peter reacts like so many doomed climbers on Everest might react to such a dramatic alteration in the environment. He becomes frantic in the face of his confusion and fear. He speeds up and does anything and everything to stay active, scurrying around collecting wood and brush to make booths.

Peter does not understand what he is experiencing on top of the mountain. It disrupts his way in the world, and, not really knowing how or why, he reacts by seeking to fill the space with his own frenetic activity. And then the cloud descends, as clouds do on mountains. Things could get worse for Peter at this point, as they often do for climbers on Everest. Peter, in his blind hurry to build huts, might walk right off the mountain.

There are those times in our lives when we feel as if we are on top of the world. We look out across the landscape and everything is clear and in its place. Work, money, family, and faith seem to click. We've all had such moments, though for most of us they are rare. What is not rare is what eventually happens on such mountaintops. Sooner or later atmospheric conditions shift. The wind whips up. Some misstep is taken, perhaps seemingly minor, and as a result confidence is lost and confusion takes over. Then, as things start to get away from us, a cloud descends and the clear view of the landscape disappears altogether. We may find ourselves lost in the fog, with all that we thought was fixed and sure swirling around us. Do you know that feeling?

Our response to such experiences is most often the response of those climbers on Everest and the response of Peter. Regardless of purpose or logic—and sometimes in the lack of either—we move. We quicken our pace, we act and react, we exhaust ourselves with pointless activity that may cause more harm than good, trying desperately to find our way in the fog that we believe threatens us so.

But what if the fog is not a threat? What if the descending cloud that overcomes us is actually a blessing sent from God? On Everest, the summit is above 29,000 feet. At 26,000 feet climbers enter what's called a "death zone" in which the oxygen becomes so thin that the body must increase its breathing from 30 breaths a minute to 80. The sheer act of breathing alone can exhaust climbers, and any pointless, superfluous activity can cause a climber suddenly to lose consciousness and even die. What if the cloud, either the literal cloud on Everest or the metaphorical cloud that can envelop our lives, is an invitation to slow down, to stop even, take shelter, listen, and wait? What if, rather than threat, the cloud intends to save our lives?

On the Mount of Transfiguration, the descending cloud causes confusion among the disciples, but then the voice of God erupts *through* the cloud, and Peter is stunned into stillness and silence and falls to the ground. God then says of Jesus, "This is my Son, the beloved, with whom I am well-pleased. Listen to him!"

Is there anything more difficult for us in our culture than to be still and listen? Especially when things are unraveling, is there anything more difficult than slowing our pace and emptying our heads of their constant, incessant buzz? We move like Peter moves. We don't slow down. We throw ourselves at problems rashly, despite the fact that in doing so we often create new problems.

We, like Peter, fear slowing down because we believe it is our activity that validates our existence. Like sharks in the ocean, we know that so long as we are moving at least we are not dead. But what if we did slow down? Are we afraid that we might not hear the voice of Christ, or are we afraid of what he might say, of what, when our lives are unraveling, he might tell us to do?

On the Mount of Transfiguration, God says to the disciples, "This is my Son." And the voice of Jesus himself follows, saying, "Rise, and do not be afraid." Once the disciples have listened, it is unavoidable that they will walk down this mountain in a direction different from where they've come, as people different from who they were when they climbed its peak.

The same it true for us. When we truly hear Jesus, he will not allow us simply to move back into the old lives that led to our unraveling. Jesus will re-ravel our lives in a new way. It is a way that points us in a new direction. It is a way that denies those things that cause our lives to fall apart—selfishness, crass ambition, materialism, prejudice of all kinds, the need to gratify every desire—and replaces them with a love so deep that it will march steadily to the cross at Calvary on our behalf. It is a way that affects everything that we are and everything that we do. It remakes us as new people.

If we take the time to be still when the cloud descends in our lives, the hand of a loving God will reach down to us. That hand will lift us up, and the voice will speak. "Rise," it will say, "Do not be afraid. Leave this life that has unraveled on the crag beneath your feet. Come down this mountain in a new direction with me, and find new life."

Amen.

Of Oaks and Kudzu

Thus says the Lord GOD: I myself will take a sprig from the lofty top of a cedar; I will set it out. I will break off a tender on from the topmost of its young twigs; I myself will plant it on a high and lofty mountain. On the mountain height of Israel I will plant it, in order that it may produce boughs and bear fruit, and become a noble cedar. Under it every kind of bird will live; in the shade of its branches will nest winged creatures of every kind. All the trees of the field shall know that I am the LORD. I bring low the high tree; I make high the low tree; I dry up the green tree and make the dry tree flourish. I the LORD have spoken; I will accomplish it.

Jesus also said, 'With what can we compare the kingdom of God, or what parable will we use for it? It is like a mustard seed, which, when sown upon the ground, is the smallest of all the seeds on earth; yet when it is sown it grows up and becomes the greatest of all shrubs, and puts forth large branches, so that the birds of the air can make nests in its shade.'

The driveway is long and straight. Stretching out from it are verdant lawns immaculately manicured. Like soldiers at attention, each blade of grass is trimmed to match its brothers. Not a dandelion is in sight. At the drive's far end rises a structure to rival the palaces of Europe. The imposing façade is marble and brick, supported by a phalanx of Corinthian columns which draw the eyes upward as if to heaven. The mansion is stately, symmetrical, and grand. But even so, it isn't the house that is most striking. Rather, what captivates the mind and the imagination is the driveway. In addition to the pristine grounds, the drive is lined on both sides by towering oak trees, aged and strong. Think Tara or her sister plantation owned by Ashley Wilkes, which was actually called "Twelve Oaks."

The layout of the drive, like the layout of a traditionally-styled church, is designed to enhance the sense of order, control, and majesty. Who from the South hasn't visited one of the old plantations—we used to visit those around Vicksburg and Natchez, Mississippi, when I was growing up—and wistfully longed for the ordered, serene and peaceful life of which they are the icon? And no part of them underscores that life more than those massive oaks.

The people of the Bible had their own version of those oak trees, and they served similarly as symbols. In Scripture, rather than Southern oaks we read about the cedars of Lebanon. Indeed, today the prophet Ezekiel uses the massive and stately cedar as the very icon of God's kingdom. Ezekiel's world is in turmoil, with his people living in exile in Babylon and their homeland destroyed. But he envisions that age when the world will finally be conformed to God's hopes and dreams for it. And what does the world of Ezekiel's dreams look like? The prophet instinctively turns to the cedar. When God's will is fulfilled, he says, it will be as if a shoot from Lebanon's greatest tree is planted on Israel's highest mountain. That new tree will grow stately and strong, until it becomes the home for every flying creature and the shade for every beast. It will bear fruit for all people. The image is the same as that of those plantation oaks: It symbolizes stability, order, majesty, and control. The fulfilled kingdom of God.

But wait a minute...Let's dig a little deeper into our cultural and iconic imagination. Take the Hermitage Plantation in Savannah, for instance. The plantation is gone, though the oak-lined drive still exists (now part of a golf course, our own century's version of manicured order). When we walk down that drive, the trees recall an age of gentility, but if we allow the eye of our imagination to pierce the scene more deeply, we may also see the eighty—yes, eighty—slave cabins that once existed in rows just beyond the oak trees. We may see the fields that existed as part of every Southern plantation, where stately majesty gave way to pitiless, back-breaking labor. We may see families torn asunder, humanity sold like chattel, people whose crippling or death was remembered not in photo albums or church memorials but on ledger sheets as the costs of business. If we look deeply, we will undoubtedly see exposed a social system that approximated heaven for those who lived in the manor house but was more like hell for everyone else.

And so, Ezekiel's image may pose a problem. It is our human tendency, then and now, to reach for symbols of strength and order, like the cedar or the oak, especially in times of turmoil. But too often we use those symbols not to point to a hoped-for future reality that all will enjoy—which is Ezekiel's intention— but rather as a screen behind which we can hide. Symbols of order and stability become images that enable us to pretend the world most of us enjoy is the real world while ignoring the depredation that exists all around us. These symbols become like those oak trees at the Hermitage Plantation, allowing us to head toward the serenity of the manor house while masking the rows of slave cabins just beyond them.

Jesus knew this. Things were not so different in his day. As an inheritor of the prophetic tradition, it would have made sense for Jesus to invoke those stately cedars of Lebanon. But instead Jesus riffs differently on Ezekiel's theme. He says, "The kingdom of God is like a *mustard seed*, which, when sown upon the ground is the smallest of all seeds; yet when it is sown it grows up and becomes the greatest of all shrubs…"

Mustard plants are not particularly common around here, so let me offer another Southern image. This one is as imbedded in our cultural psyches as that of the plantation, maybe more so these days. In the late 1800s a plant was imported to the United States from Japan as an effective prevention against soil erosion, and by 1935 the Soil Conservation Service was encouraging Southern farmers to plant this botanical miracle with abandon. Bad idea. Within a couple of decades, the plant became known as "the vine that ate the South." It had a tendency to spread beyond the borders of where it was desired. It had a bad habit of overtaking anything in its path, fields, trees, you name it—a sort of horticultural "Blob". It was unpredictable, impossible to contain, and extremely difficult to kill once it had taken root. You, of course, know what I'm talking about: Kudzu.

Kudzu gives us an idea of what Jesus means when he talks about the mustard plant. Mustard was wild, scraggly, a nuisance. Beginning as just a tiny seed, it could erupt almost overnight into something that could not be contained. Unlike the stately and rooted cedar, the mustard plant would spread out and change the entire landscape. It bore no respect for manicured gardens, overwhelming them with its disordered growth.

The oaks along plantation drives should rightly fear kudzu. Just so, the stately and ordered—but also veneer-thin—majesty of this world should rightly fear the kingdom of God. The kingdom, when it takes hold, grows in unpredictable and uncontrollable ways. It changes the landscape entirely. Have you seen it? Have you ever been in a place where the kingdom has taken root? Like kudzu, the presence of God spreads out and overwhelms every icon, every idol. Suddenly, where there was peace, peace is shattered. Where there was decorum and order, disorder reigns. And yet, the change is so obviously a blessing! When God's love grows, people trample the grass; they plow over the oaks, and they spread that life-giving vine to all those who have never enjoyed peace, comfort, and stability, who have never known the inside of the manor house.

This is true in spiritual ways and in material ways. Where the kingdom of God grows, good people give up their manor house pretensions and give: of themselves, of their prayer, of the material blessings they enjoy. They labor in love to change the very landscape of the world, to offer the mustard plant's solace, protection, and shade to anyone in their path.

And just as this is true in the world, it's also true in the soul. We hide behind images of stability and order within us, too. Within, we struggle mightily to arrange stately oaks so that we can avoid the turmoil—emotional, psychological, spiritual—that churns just beyond the trees. But the kingdom can grow within, too!

There is that wonderful chapter in Paul Young's *The Shack* in which the main character, Mack, is taken by the Holy Spirit into a wild and aromatic garden: a garden of flowers, herbs like mustard, and, we can imagine, kudzu.[1] He is struck that the garden is so much more beautiful, so much more brimming with life than the artificial and sculpted gardens he knows in his life. Slowly Mack realizes that the garden in which he walks with God's Spirit is his soul. Slowly as the novel wears on, it is the wild growth in that garden, allowed to expand freely, that overcomes the deep hurt and the turmoil Mack knows.

If we'll open the gate even an inch to the kingdom of God in the world and in our souls, its growth will amaze us. But don't think it will grow in a stately and ordered way, rooted to one spot. In the church and in our own hearts it will overrun us. It'll be scary (like the movie *The Blob* was scary), but it will also overcome our deepest hurts and those of the world.

Here in this place, may we see beyond the oak trees, and may kudzu abound.

Amen.

ENDNOTES

1 William P. Young, *The Shack* (Newbury Park, CA: Windblown Media, 2008), 128.

Dropping the Shovel

OCTOBER 2010   GENESIS 32:22-31

The same night he got up and took his two wives, his two maids, and his eleven children, and crossed the ford of the Jabbok. He took them and sent them across the stream, and likewise everything that he had. Jacob was left alone; and a man wrestled with him until daybreak. When the man saw that he did not prevail against Jacob, he struck him on the hip socket; and Jacob's hip was put out of joint as he wrestled with him. Then he said, 'Let me go, for the day is breaking.' But Jacob said, 'I will not let you go, unless you bless me.' So he said to him, 'What is your name?' And he said, 'Jacob.' Then the man said, 'You shall no longer be called Jacob, but Israel, for you have striven with God and with humans, and have prevailed.' Then Jacob asked him, 'Please tell me your name.' But he said, 'Why is it that you ask my name?' And there he blessed him. So Jacob called the place Peniel, saying, 'For I have seen God face to face, and yet my life is preserved.' The sun rose upon him as he passed Peniel, limping because of his hip.

The thirty-three Chilean men were accustomed to digging their way out of tough situations. They were miners, after all. Darkness, dust, cold, and heat to which most of us would quickly succumb were a daily part of life for them. They handled extreme pressures both under and above the ground. One had been a national soccer star. He'd navigated the intense pressures of the fans and the field for an entire career before plunging into the dark earth of the mine. Another had walked, in his surface life, the tightrope of keeping both a wife and family and a mistress. He'd shuttled and juggled between two lives for so long that he'd made an art of it. It seemed there was nothing that these hardy men couldn't dig out from under if only they applied enough effort.

So when their mine exploded one August day, they didn't panic. After the initial dust settled, they gathered together and moved toward the 2,300 foot safety ladder that was supposed to take them all the way to the surface. They began to climb out of the hole they had dug, but a third of the way up, the ladder hit solid rock and stopped. It had never been completed, just one of many human failings that plagued the Chilean mining disaster. As the lead miner on the top rung of the ladder felt the smooth rock above his head, he and the others realized that they finally found themselves in a life situation they perhaps dimly feared would one day come. They were trapped in the darkness, in a hole out of which they were powerless to dig.

In Genesis Jacob—who also knows a bit about ladders—finds himself in similar straits. Jacob, too, has led a life in which he can dig his way out of anything. Indeed, he has learned again and again that, with enough conniving, effort, and force of will there is nothing he can't earn or attain.

It helps to recap Jacob's life briefly. He was born second to his twin Esau in an age when the first-born received the father's only blessing. But a second-fiddle life wasn't acceptable to Jacob. He realized that to gain a share of the blessing, he'd have to beg, borrow, or steal. He began to dig. First he preyed upon his brother's fatigue and hunger to trade a bowl of soup for Esau's birthright. Later, he preyed upon his father's age and blindness to trick Isaac into thinking Jacob was Esau and bestow his blessing on the wrong son. Jacob always digs his way to the top.

The theme repeats itself again and again. Jacob works to earn the love of Leah and Rachel. He connives to gain half the wealth of his uncle Laban. He digs and digs and digs, and he learns that there is no hole into which he can be trapped.

That is, until today. Just prior to our reading, Jacob has decided to return home after more than twenty years away. He'd fled home in fear of his life after stealing Esau's blessing. Jacob's return journey reminds me of the great line from the film *The Myth of Fingerprints* when the psychiatrist asks Warren why, after three long years, he's making a trip home. Warren replies, "Because it's been just long enough that I can't remember why I shouldn't go."

But the closer he gets, the more the reality of home comes crashing back upon him. As Esau has headed out to meet him, Jacob remembers the pain he's caused, and—even though it's what's put him in this mess in the first place, he starts digging! He sends toward Esau wave upon wave of servants and material wealth, believing he can—through pay off, effort, and force of will—once again find himself on top. But as today's reading begins, word has arrived that Esau is still coming Jacob's direction, now with four hundred men in tow. It is as if Jacob has reached the top rung of an incomplete escape ladder. He's hit a rock wall. He's alone. Darkness has fallen. And there's absolutely nothing he can do for himself.

The Chilean miners endured two full weeks in the darkness of the mine, a half mile distant from the light of the sun, before any contact at all was made with the world on the surface. I get nervous when the elevator door is delayed in opening. I can't imagine what it must have been like trapped in that hole. When contact was finally made, the men received the devastating word that two more months would pass before their rescue could occur. Then, finally this past Wednesday the men were slowly and laboriously—one per hour—lifted from the bowels of the earth.

At some point, the thirty-three miners recognized, accepted, and ultimately embraced the reality that they found themselves in a situation from which they could not dig out. They had to come to terms with the fact that their effort, intelligence, and force of will were powerless. What must that have felt like? One miner shed some light when he reached the surface this week. "We spent the last ten weeks in the darkness between God and the devil," he said, "and God won."

That's a description of a wrestling match, one in which the devil whispers in one ear all those futile things the miners should do to effect their own rescue and God whispers in the other that there is nothing they can do, that they must wait upon salvation from another, that they must receive grace. And God won.

It is the same wrestling match Jacob experiences in the darkness. He searches for a solution, for anything he can do *to work his way out* of the hole he has dug. And God responds from the darkness...by throwing Jacob to the ground, slapping him around, doing whatever God must for Jacob to recognize, accept, and finally embrace that there is *nothing* he can do to effect his own rescue. There is no conniving, no alternate route, no ransom to be paid. Jacob is powerless, and the only way to prevail is to rely upon God's blessing and grace. It is a gift he cannot earn but is given to him anyway. You see, even in deepest darkness God will not leave Jacob alone, and whatever Jacob must face, they will face together.

There is more to Jacob's story. He survives his meeting with Esau, a meeting that actually turns out better than he can ask or imagine. But it is so because Jacob relies upon the grace of God and not his own shovel.

Jacob is dazed by this grace. He will limp under its blessed weight. The Chilean miners were equally dazed. On the earth's surface this past Wednesday some of them jumped like schoolchildren, others gazed awestruck upon their loved ones, and some dropped to their knees making the sign of the cross in thanksgiving.

In ways subtle and overt, we—like Jacob—learn even from childhood how to dig our way out of any mess, how to get on top through conniving, effort, and force of will, how to earn the love we covet. Too often, though, this strategy for life leaves us in the darkness. Living with self-centered short-sightedness, when we think we're digging to the top we're only making the hole deeper. The escape ladder fails to reach the light and is stopped short by unyielding rock. Success eludes us. We hurt those we should love. And we find ourselves mired in anxiety, guilt, and a sense of failure. This will never change unless and until in our wrestling against God we admit our powerlessness, unless and until we cease our panicked striving and instead wait upon grace. Of that grace, Brennan Manning says:

> "[Through grace] we have the power to believe where others deny, to hope where others despair, to love where others hurt. [But] this and so much more is sheer gift; it is not reward for our faithfulness, our generous disposition, or our heroic life of prayer...My deepest awareness of myself is that I am deeply loved by Jesus Christ and I have done nothing to earn or deserve it."[1]

Like the men and women who worked ceaselessly to reach those thirty-three miners trapped 2300 feet underground, God works ceaselessly upon us, chinking through the stony walls to embrace us with empowering grace. God will wrestle with us; he will prod and push and challenge *because, despite whatever holes we've dug ourselves into, God loves us with a love that is freely given.*

Of course, grace doesn't mean that all life's problems melt away. As one example, upon reaching the surface one miner must still respond to the shattering pain caused by his infidelity. But the manner in which we address any of life's circumstances becomes different when addressed through God's grace. Instead of digging to preserve ourselves, we respond as recipients of God's great gift. We own our faults, we put the care of others before our own, we relish the occasions where God's presence is felt rather than harping on passing moments of darkness.

Dropping our futile shovels and returning God's embrace, we find ourselves lifted out of the hole. We can jump around like schoolchildren; we can gaze in wonder at those we love; we can drop to our knees and make the sign of the cross. We will live our lives in a new way, in gracious response to this most gracious gift.

Amen.

Endnotes

1 Brennan Manning, *The Ragamuffin Gospel*, 3rd ed. (Colorado Springs, CO: Multnomah Books, 2005), 25.

Searching for the Pole

MARCH 2011   MATTHEW 10:5-15

These twelve Jesus sent out with the following instructions: 'Go nowhere among the Gentiles, and enter no town of the Samaritans, but go rather to the lost sheep of the house of Israel. As you go, proclaim the good news, "The kingdom of heaven has come near." Cure the sick, raise the dead, cleanse the lepers, cast out demons. You received without payment; give without payment. Take no gold, or silver, or copper in your belts, no bag for your journey, or two tunics, or sandals, or a staff; for laborers deserve their food. Whatever town or village you enter, find out who in it is worthy, and stay there until you leave. As you enter the house, greet it. If the house is worthy, let your peace come upon it; but if it is not worthy, let your peace return to you. If anyone will not welcome you or listen to your words, shake off the dust from your feet as you leave that house or town. Truly I tell you, it will be more tolerable for the land of Sodom and Gomorrah on the day of judgment than for that town.

I was born and raised in the Eastern Arkansas delta, and four years ago I moved to the Blue Ridge Mountains. When you're from a flat part of the world and you move to the mountains, your friends from home begin to think of you as adventuresome, as some sort of Indiana Jones-type character. They call and e-mail with questions about the caverns I must have explored, the trails I must have hiked, the mountains I must have climbed. I try to explain that the only slice of the Roanoke Valley that I've traversed with any regularity is the two-mile stretch of Jefferson Street between the church and my house, but to no avail. To my friends, I'm an adventurer.

A couple of weeks ago I decided if my friends were going to keep up this illusion the least I can do is speak knowledgably. So I picked up Bill Bryson's bestselling book *A Walk in the Woods*, which chronicles his attempt to hike the entire Appalachian Trail. That adventure made me think of other famous treks—my mind tends to work that way—and I started reading about men and women who have explored the more famous spots on the globe. All such stories are fascinating, but the ones that captivated me most were the expeditions to the North Pole.

Despite the extreme difficulties associated with a trek to the Pole (more about those later), one would think that *finding* the thing is a simple affair. You head due north, and sooner or later you'll reach it. Not so, it turns out. There are myriad problems locating the North Pole, so many that the debate continues to rage about who has actually found it and who has not.

The first problem is that, unlike the South Pole which is covered by the Antarctic landmass, there is no land over the North Pole. There is only sea ice, and sea ice continually moves. In other words, if one, by virtue of compasses, global positioning systems, or a good old thumb-in-the-air, does locate the North Pole and thrust a flag into the ice, within hours or even minutes the ice may shift, and as soon as the Pole has been found it is gone.

But there's an even bigger problem. The North Pole is defined as that point where the axis of the earth's rotation meets the earth's surface. If, like the spoke of a wheel, the earth's axis were fixed, then we could—at least on our instruments— find the Pole with exact specificity. But it's not fixed, it turns out. For reasons unknown, the earth's axis wobbles, and the precise North Pole doesn't stand still.

Not only the ice covering it, but the Pole itself shifts and moves. So again, just when the intrepid explorer thinks he's found the Pole, he may realize that he's in fact standing on just another ordinary, cold and barren spot on earth.

Have people, then, given up seeking the North Pole? Not by a long shot. But those who make the journey with wisdom do so knowing that the best they'll be able to do in their search to find the Pole is to skim its edges. They know that—like trying to reach the horizon—the Pole is forever elusive. It beckons and lures, and the closer one's approach, the more palpable its *power*...but also its *mystery*. The Pole won't be pinned like a moth on a corkboard. It won't be *known* in any sort of direct, definitive, exhaustive way.

How like God! And how like us. We human beings continually set out in search of the divine, usually prompted by the same motivations that lure adventurers to the woods, or the mountains, or the North Pole. These motivations are legion. We may experience an emptiness and a sense that the God somewhere out there can fill it. We may perceive a power beyond us, pulsating and awesome, and an irresistible urge to move toward it. Or we may hear a voice, like someone whispering to us, barely audible above the din of life, calling us out and onto the well-trodden path.

Today, the followers of Jesus head out onto the path. They are sent on expedition by Jesus himself, to seek God and along the way to invite others to travel with them. Jesus is very particular about the way he outfits this expedition. He tells the disciples what they can and cannot take on their journey with them. They are to travel light, and instead of the comforts of home, they are to carry with them tasks and proclamations. "Cure the sick,' Jesus says, "Raise the dead; cast out demons; and declare that God's kingdom has come near."

In my recent reading, the other thing that has been of tantalizing interest is the way in which various polar explorers have outfitted themselves. Annie Dillard describes the 1845 Franklin expedition, in which Sir John Franklin and 138 British officers and men headed north to find the Pole and the Northwest Passage.[1] They expected their trip to be quick and direct, and they ladened their ships with what they considered all the important provisions for their quest to find the Pole. This didn't include fur coats or extra coal for warmth, but these proper, nineteenth century British explorers *did* include a 1200-volume library, a hand organ to play merry tunes, china place settings for all the men, cut-glass wine goblets, and sterling silver flatware.

When winter set in, as it was bound to, the ships of the Franklin expedition quickly became stuck in the icepack. Once it became evident that there was no chance of breaking free, the men disembarked the ship and headed out across the ice, hoping for any salvation. They carried with them those things they believed to be essential provisions. Bodies were later found weighted down with engraved silver flatware, a backgammon board, and lots of tea. Often they were found dressed to the hilt in their thin but finest naval uniforms of blue trousers and jackets.

When the explorers of the Franklin expedition sought the elusive North Pole, they set out half-baked and poorly provisioned. And though they were undoubtedly surprised at their own swift demise—I can imagine them absurdly sipping tea on an ice floe as they froze in their thin uniforms—we should not be. How they set about their search and what they chose to take with them could never get them to their destination.

The same is true of our quest for God. God cannot be approached quickly or directly. Some will say they have located God, and with the same certainty that they find their way from home to work. Whether individuals or churches, some will say they have staked their flag with sure and complete knowledge of who God is. They'll presume to pin God like a moth to corkboard and utter truisms about him as if God were a specimen subject to our examination.

And then the ice shifts. The Pole wobbles. And it's gone. Sooner or later in life, the pinned-down God is revealed to be as elusive as the North Pole itself. He'll defy our expectations and disrupt our lives, and those who have claimed to have pegged him with certainty may find that they stand on just another cold, barren, and lonely chunk of ice.

How then are we to make this expedition? How are we to seek God? The first key is to acknowledge that it will not be done quickly or casually. The Franklin expedition saw theirs as one of speed and ease. The expedition toward God will only be made with commitment of heart, soul, and time. We must orient ourselves to the journey, in contemplation, prayer, and a reordering of our whole lives (not just the occasional hour on a Sunday morning).

The second key is to acknowledge the limits to what we, as human beings, can know of God. God is not a prize to be captured (and thank God for that).

He will not be known fully and directly. At our very best, we can approach God—as wise explorers approach the North Pole—only around the edges. We can sense when we move closer or further from him, and in the briefest of instances we may experience his nearness as if he is right under our feet, but we must also acknowledge that the mystery of God is fathomless. He'll surprise us and challenge us and lure us in directions we least expect. And the experience that comes from approaching this elusive God—more like experiencing beauty or love than knowing an object—is far more fulfilling and abiding than the superficial satisfaction one has with knowing a caricature of God that ultimately leaves us in the cold.

And the final key is how we outfit for the journey. We chuckle and raise a knowing eyebrow at the Victorians of the Franklin expedition, but we, too, risk setting out on our quest with unhelpful and ultimately worthless baubles. We give priority to the spit and polish uniforms and the engraved flatware that define our world. We encumber and surround ourselves with these things, giving precedence of our time, our money, and our waking thoughts not to the things that ready us to know God, but to the things the world says have value. What little good such things were to the Franklin expedition! What little good they are to us.

We will only find the approach to God when we un-encumber our lives. We will only discover the passage when we heed the words of Jesus to loose those things by which the world defines us. In place of china and crystal, the Franklin expedition should have carried fur and coal for life-giving warmth. In our lives, we need only the warmth that comes from the mission given us by Jesus. Like the disciples, we need only go forth believing, declaring and living as if the kingdom of God—the new world of grace—is near. We need only set out on the path with words of love and hope that cleanse those who feel dirty in the world, that cast out the demons who plague lives. Then we'll sense it. We'll know we are close. The ice will break apart, and we will find ourselves around the very edges of the heart of God.

Amen.

ENDNOTES

1 Annie Dillard, *Teaching a Stone to Talk* (New York: HarperCollins, 1982), 29-64.

Water

Letting Go

MARCH 2004   GENESIS 15:1-12, 17-21

After these things the word of the LORD came to Abram in a vision, 'Do not be afraid, Abram, I am your shield; your reward shall be very great.' But Abram said, 'O Lord GOD, what will you give me, for I continue childless, and the heir of my house is Eliezer of Damascus?' And Abram said, 'You have given me no offspring, and so a slave born in my house is to be my heir.' But the word of the LORD came to him, 'This man shall not be your heir; no one but your very own issue shall be your heir.' He brought him outside and said, 'Look towards heaven and count the stars, if you are able to count them.' Then he said to him, 'So shall your descendants be.' And he believed the LORD; and the LORD reckoned it to him as righteousness.

Then he said to him, 'I am the LORD who brought you from Ur of the Chaldeans, to give you this land to possess.' But he said, 'O Lord GOD, how am I to know that I shall possess it?' He said to him, 'Bring me a heifer three years old, a female goat three years old, a ram three years old, a turtle-dove, and a young pigeon.' He brought him all these and cut them in two, laying each half over against the other; but he did not cut the birds in two. And when birds of prey came down on the carcasses, Abram drove them away. *As the sun was going down, a deep sleep fell upon Abram, and a deep and terrifying darkness descended upon him.*

When the sun had gone down and it was dark, a smoking fire-pot and a flaming torch passed between these pieces. On that day the LORD made a covenant with Abram, saying, 'To your descendants I give this land, from the river of Egypt to the great river, the river Euphrates, the land of the Kenites, the Kenizzites, the Kadmonites, the Hittites, the Perizzites, the Rephaim, the Amorites, the Canaanites, the Girgashites, and the Jebusites.'

◊

Have you spent any time in the Ozarks in the summer time? If you haven't, you're missing out on one of life's great joys. I can't count the number of days in the first eighteen years of my life I spent camping and canoeing in that gorgeous territory. You almost have to have driven there yourself to appreciate the beauty. The Arkansas delta, where I was raised, is so flat that one can almost see where it drops off. The most remarkable change in scenery is when the bean fields give way to cotton. But head West, and the ground under the car begins to rise. Soon, your ears pop a little. Foliage becomes thicker, and the summer humidity begins to cling to the leaves of every tree overhanging the increasingly winding highway. You've moved into the Ozark foothills.

But I need to make this trip more particular, more personal. It was the summer of 1996. My wife Jill and I had been married scarcely a year. We'd escaped a family reunion in Paragould, and were headed to Hardy, Arkansas, for a day of canoeing on the Spring River.

There's something you need to know about the mountain rivers in Arkansas. They are deceptive streams. In places they look placid, but they rarely are. Even when the surface appears to be still as glass, just beneath there is a powerful current. These rivers are spring fed, and an incredible volume of water is pushed downhill through shallow channels with rock bottoms. This confluence of factors creates eddies, undertows, and the occasional drop off that can take one by surprise. What's more, as a river meanders through the hills, the channel sometimes divides, other times narrows, so that the water is shot forward as though through a firehose.

But on this August day in 1996, the river was heaven, and I knew it like the back of my hand. We moved along laughing, taking on the rapids with gusto, Jill steering and me powering through the dicey areas. I pointed out landmarks I remembered, and generally tried to impress my newlywed bride with my skill and prowess in taming the stream. So much fun we were having, that we didn't notice a logjam ahead at a point where the channel divided. At the fork, the main channel was the only safe one. The smaller, right hand tributary was trecherous. But today, the main channel was blocked. A party of raucous canoers had bunched up and overturned, and they were taking their drunken time getting out of the way. I saw a couple of people head to the right to avoid this mess, and I told Jill to follow suit.

The next few minutes are still a blur. Just ahead of us, a canoe had front-ended the fork's first rapid, filled with water, and flipped end-over. As soon as I realized what had happened, I shoved my paddle into the river bottom and turned us sideways. Bad idea. With our weight on the back side of the canoe, the rapid slung us over broadside. I was dimly aware that the canoe was now wedged upside down across the narrow channel. The cold water was shock-inducing, and the current swift and unrelenting. I didn't know where Jill was. In a desperate attempt to regain my equilibrium, my hands were clinging to the back lip of the boat. The water couldn't have been more than two and a half feet deep, but my scrambling feet couldn't gain hold of the bottom. My arms strained to pull my nose and mouth above water, but with each effort I was able to hoist myself less and less, never once getting above the surface.

In a matter of seconds, a world that had been nothing but beauty and fun— heaven, really—was transformed into hell. I had been sure in my knowledge of my surroundings, sure of my abilities to navigate my path, and sure of my power to do so with success and safety. There'd been no doubt. And now, I realized, I was drowning. As consciousness began to fade, a deep and terrifying darkness fell upon me.

I guess the greatest irony about my situation was that the river wasn't killing me; my struggle was. I was straining with every ounce of strength I had to pull my self backward and up against the current. Any second, my lungs would demand that I open my mouth seeking oxygen, and all they would receive would be deadly water.

What saved me was that my strength gave out. Before my mouth opened to suck in water, my hands gave way, releasing the lip of the canoe. Instantly, the river became my savior. It whipped me under the canoe, bobbed me to the surface, and darted me through the rapid channel to the calmer water beyond. I crawled up the bank, head aching and shin sliced, and hurried breathlessly back to where the canoe was still lodged. There against a tree leaned Jill, wet but safe and looking around for me.

I hadn't thought about that frightening event for years until I read the Old Testament lesson for today. With all the political rancor in our country, with all the debate in The Episcopal Church, with all the trials facing our families, we share a collective desire to fix it all: clean it up, clear out all the ambiguity, cover the current with a placid surface. Abram shared our desire and our struggle. When I meditated on his experience and on our own, my harrowing event on the Spring River became a potent metaphor.

Abram was not an unfaithful man. By the time we get to today's passage in Genesis, he has already followed the call of God to leave his homeland and enter into uncharted territory. But Abram has also shown a troubling tendency to put himself on par with God, to assume that he knows better than God how to get himself through life's desperate situations. In one instance, when a famine plagues his land, Abram takes his wife down to Egypt to buy food. Sarai his wife is beautiful, and Abram fears that some Egyptian will kill him in order to take her as his wife. So Abram pretends that Sarai is his sister. Sure enough, in Egypt he runs into Pharaoh himself and Pharaoh lusts after Sarai's beauty. Since Abram presents his wife as his sister, Pharaoh takes her into his house as his own mistress. In Abram's attempt to save his own skin, he ends up prostituting his wife, whose honor he ought to have protected! In other words, his struggle to control life's circumstances made things worse than they would have been otherwise.

But in today's reading, God initiates a new relationship with Abram. God says, "Do not be afraid. I am your shield." Yet, fear is something to which we cling—like clinging to the lip of an overturned boat—and Abram can't let go. He immediately begins to plot, plan and negotiate with God. "God," he says, "You've given me no heir, no one to take care of me in old age. Now let's see, I've got to come up with a back up plan. I'm going to have to leave all of my possessions to one of my servants and…"

God interrupts Abram's chatter. "No one but your own child shall be your heir," God promises, "Your descendents will be more numerous than the stars, and this land will be yours to possess."

Still Abram cannot let go of his fear. "How do I know you'll keep your word?" he pleads. And showing pity on a weak and frightened man, God formalizes a covenant with Abram. He has Abram gather sacrificial animals, but the man's effort exhausts him, and we are told that "a deep sleep fell upon Abram, and a deep and terrifying darkness descended upon him."

Sleeping, Abram cannot continue to cling to his fear. He can't struggle. He lets go, and as he sleeps, God seals the covenant. God moves among the sacrificial animals and commits to keep Abram and his descendents in divine care for all eternity. And here's the wondrous thing about God's covenant: It is grace. God asks nothing of Abram but his faith. All Abram must do is remain in faithful relationship with God and let go, give up on his own efforts to secure, protect, and fix his world—quit struggling against God and allow God to carry him forward in love. It's a hard lesson to learn, and Abram doesn't learn it immediately. But he's on his way. Grace has moved underneath him to bear him along, bob him to the surface, and it will not let him down.

How often life's tranquility can turn on a dime, throwing at us things terrifying: eddies and undertows and drop-offs. Life's placid surface gives way to a relentless current underneath! Our first instinct is to struggle and to fix things right, and in some instances this is exactly what we should do. But there are those other times, when the world's, or the church's, or the family's circumstances are beyond our control and ability to repair, and in those times there is wisdom in surrender. Yet, we must always be aware that it is not the world toward which we give in. Rather, it is into God that we let go, buoyed with hope in our covenant with Christ Jesus. This doesn't mean that we'll float through life injury-free. But when we give up our struggle and relax into the presence of God, we can be assured that God will bear us aloft in love, and we can weather life's trials, scrapes and all.

Amen.

Giving Up the Great Catch

FEBRUARY 2007

LUKE 5:1-11

Once while Jesus was standing beside the lake of Gennesaret, and the crowd was pressing in on him to hear the word of God, he saw two boats there at the shore of the lake; the fishermen had gone out of them and were washing their nets. He got into one of the boats, the one belonging to Simon, and asked him to put out a little way from the shore. Then he sat down and taught the crowds from the boat. When he had finished speaking, he said to Simon, 'Put out into the deep water and let down your nets for a catch.' Simon answered, 'Master, we have worked all night long but have caught nothing. Yet if you say so, I will let down the nets.' When they had done this, they caught so many fish that their nets were beginning to break. So they signalled to their partners in the other boat to come and help them. And they came and filled both boats, so that they began to sink. But when Simon Peter saw it, he fell down at Jesus' knees, saying, 'Go away from me, Lord, for I am a sinful man!' For he and all who were with him were amazed at the catch of fish that they had taken; and so also were James and John, sons of Zebedee, who were partners with Simon. Then Jesus said to Simon, 'Do not be afraid; from now on you will be catching people.' When they had brought their boats to shore, they left everything and followed him.

Billy Tyne was a fisherman. I don't mean that he was one who liked to spend a casual day on the water. Billy Tyne was one of those whose life was truly defined and consumed by being on the water. He lived in the cold environs of Massachusetts. He was weathered and lined from the wind and the chill. Whenever on land, he had that distant look and that sense of obsessive urgency, always thinking ahead to the next catch, which was surely to be the big one. That's what led Billy Tyne back out to sea with his crew on his swordfish boat, the Andrea Gail, in the latter half of October 1991.

In late October 1991, a hurricane and two other violent storm systems joined together off the New England coast in an unholy marriage unlike any other in recorded history. Meteorologists didn't know what to make of it. Author Sebastian Junger and later Warner Brothers Films called it, "The Perfect Storm."

Two weeks out, Billy Tyne knew that something was brewing in the several hundred miles between his boat and the shore, but he also knew that he had just had the catch of his life. His crew had pulled a quarter million dollars worth of swordfish out of the deep after a season-long dry spell, but no sooner had they filled the hold than the boat's refrigeration system failed. If Billy Tyne rode around the storm, the fish would spoil. He had to get to shore; he had to have his fish. This haul was his whole life. It was everything he had dreamed and hoped for. Nothing was more important.

Within hours after heading headlong into the Perfect Storm, the *Andrea Gail* broke apart and settled onto the bottom of the ocean, taking her entire crew with her. Billy Tyne would not leave his catch. He would not let go. And he died to the depths.

Simon Peter is a fisherman. I think we forget that. He's not some guy who enjoys fishing. He is a *fisherman*. And if we want a potent image of what that means, then we could do worse than to consider the salty and obsessive Billy Tyne.

Keep that in mind now, as we consider Jesus walking along the banks of the Sea of Galilee today. It is morning, and the fishermen who have just returned from night fishing are washing their nets. Knowing what Scripture tells us of Simon's nature, there's little doubt that he has that distant, urgent look in his eyes, that he is already thinking longingly about the next launch. Maybe it startles him as he turns around from picking seaweed from his nets to see Jesus climbing aboard his boat. Thankfully for our children's tender ears, Luke doesn't record what were probably Simon's first salty words in Jesus' direction. Whatever Simon says, Jesus ignores him and, after teaching the gathered crowd, tells Simon to go out again into the deep water and drop the nets. What to do? Throw Jesus overboard, or call his bluff? Simon chooses the latter. He heads back out into deep water, and as soon as the sloop drops its nets again, he feels that tell-tale sensation of the boat's weight adjusting as the nets fill with fish.

And oh, the fish! The nets fill quickly to capacity, and for once the distance in Simon's eyes gives way to amazement. He's never seen so many fish. It's the kind of haul that can make all the difference in the life of a man like Simon. To use an apt metaphor, Simon's ship has come in.

Simon is a fisherman. It is who he is. He looks at the nets, full to bursting, and he looks at Jesus who is moving on. *Remember Billy Tyne.* This haul is Simon's whole life. It is everything he has dreamed and hoped for. With the choice in front of him—the great catch or the Way of Jesus—he is confronted with a temptation at least as great as the ones Satan put before Jesus himself. Simon takes a last look at the fish, but now the distance he has known his whole adult life disappears forever from his eyes. In the fish, he has finally seen the future he's always wanted, but in Jesus he sees something he'd have scarcely imagined possible. He leaves the fish—his great haul—and he leaves the boat to follow Jesus.

Of the people in Billy Tyne's life, only Christina, the girlfriend of Billy's first mate Bobby, truly understands the fishermen. "Another trip and the *Andrea Gale* will own you," she warns her boyfriend, "like she owns Billy Tyne."

Christina is the only one who intuitively grasps the danger facing the *Andrea Gale*. It is not the weather. Weather always comes up; deadly storms of one sort or another are not uncommon. The real danger is in grasping something so hard that, before you know it, it grasps you. It owns you. Billy Tyne has come to belong to the great catch, not the other way round. He wants it so bad and has followed it for so long that it owns him, and it takes him with it into the depths.

Though none of us are fishermen in the sense of Billy Tyne or Simon, we know what it is to have that distant look in our eyes, to be so invested in a way of life or a heart's desire that it consumes us. The drives in our lives—some we cherish, some we despise—sooner or later threaten to own us. Everything and everyone else in our lives are given over to the great catch, and whatever doesn't help us fill the nets is pushed aside or discarded altogether.

But here's the real catch (to use a sorry pun): Both Simon and Billy Tyne die. Billy Tyne dies because he will not let go of the great catch even to save his life. But Simon dies by giving up his life, by leaving behind the very thing that has defined him, in favor of the promise of a way of being that will make even his bursting nets pale in comparison. Simon dies so that he might live; Billy Tyne dies for a stack of dead fish.

Most often, when we're out in the fishing boats of our lives (whatever those may be), pursuing the great catch with such unassailable determination that it comes to own us, it is only the outsider who can look in upon us and recognize how skewed our priorities are. Luke, who tells us today's story of Jesus and Simon, makes this very point, but we almost miss it. Simon sets his gaze daily on the Sea of Galilee, but Luke is a world traveler. He's seen the *real* ocean, and he laughs at the idea that this body of water upon which the disciples fish is a "sea".[1] Unlike the other evangelists, who talk constantly of the Sea of Galilee, Luke calls it, instead, the "Lake of Gennesaret", as if to say that this puddle of a pond in which Simon toils is nothing compared to the Way of Jesus he will follow.

The same is true for us. The priorities that consume us are often comical, sometimes grotesquely so. The oceans' horizons that own us, causing us to disregard or discard all other things of value in our lives are, when we take a step back, revealed to be little more than brackish ponds. And so we're left with the choice: we can either throw that catch overboard and sail a new direction, or we can sink into the darkness of the depths.

That's why we miss everything if we fail to understand that *Simon Peter is a fisherman!* He, as much or more than any one of us, is driven and obsessed with the great catch. And yet even with the nets full to bursting, he sets his sights away from the water and squarely upon Jesus the Christ. That is the Gospel message with which we are left this day: God in heaven and in our hearts gives us a permission that is so unexpected that we can scarcely bring ourselves to believe it: *There is no such thing as being so far down a path, so invested in a way of being, that we cannot drop it overboard, turn around, and follow a new direction.*

We can tie up to the dock; we can get off the boat; we can follow the Way. Make no mistake. In doing so we, too, will die. But the death that we die will not be to the depths. It will be death to that distant look and obsessive striving. It will be new life in Christ.

Amen.

ENDNOTES

1 M. Eugene Boring and Fred B. Craddock, *The People's New Testament Commentary* (Louisville, KY: Westminster John Knox Press, 2004), 194.

The Family of God

NOVEMBER 2007 LUKE 20:27-38

Some Sadducees, those who say there is no resurrection, came to Jesus and asked him a question, 'Teacher, Moses wrote for us that if a man's brother dies, leaving a wife but no children, the man shall marry the widow and raise up children for his brother. Now there were seven brothers; the first married, and died childless; then the second and the third married her, and so in the same way all seven died childless. Finally the woman also died. In the resurrection, therefore, whose wife will the woman be? For the seven had married her.'

Jesus said to them, 'Those who belong to this age marry and are given in marriage; but those who are considered worthy of a place in that age and in the resurrection from the dead neither marry nor are given in marriage. Indeed they cannot die any more, because they are like angels and are children of God, being children of the resurrection. And the fact that the dead are raised Moses himself showed, in the story about the bush, where he speaks of the Lord as the God of Abraham, the God of Isaac, and the God of Jacob. Now he is God not of the dead, but of the living; for to him all of them are alive.'

◊

Those summers at the state park in Walcott, Arkansas, always began awkwardly. We gathered on the even-numbered years, and we would rent the entire campground, with six or eight cabins and a dining hall at the top of the hill. Officially, this was the bi-annual reunion of my grandmother's people. She was one of nine children, and during the Depression the siblings had scattered to Alabama, Louisiana, and Indiana. Children had children who had children, and by the time I was a kid there were scores of us. With our presence, the state park was transformed into something different, a gathering place for what I was told was *my family*.

When we arrived, my mother would get us out of the car, lick her finger and rub the dirt off of my face (I hated that), and walk us up to the nearest stranger to say, "This is your Uncle Pete with the wooden leg," or, "These are the Demskis. You remember, from Birmingham. Little Ray is in the Navy."

I remember that I was terrified by that wooden leg, and I had trouble pronouncing "Demski." But what I most recall is standing frozen in place, with a beehive of activity swirling all around me. No one looked like me. The Indiana relatives were burly and red-haired. Some of them drove to Walcott on motorcycles, and they had tattoos of things I couldn't understand...and was probably better off not understanding! And then there were our kin who drove up from Louisiana. One year the Louisiana kids came without their parents, and I'm pretty sure the oldest child was not of legal driving age. I would bet that he had to put blocks on the gas pedal just to reach it.

As I stood in the middle of this melee, frozen in place, I would think to myself, "This is my *family?*"

But as the week went on, something unusual happened. The crazy and petrifying menagerie first became familiar, then welcome, and finally something I embraced as my own. People ate and played together. We told stories and shared our hopes and pains. We began to love one another, and our love would abide even at week's end when we would pile into our cars (or onto our Harleys in some cases) and go our separate ways. We would carry that love with us, and it added a depth to our lives that was not there before.

When did it happen? When did this mismatched group of people connected by the most distant blood ties become a true family? I believe it was that first time we stripped down to our cut-off jeans and dove into the waters of Walcott Lake. There was always in that moment a transformation of sorts, when we let go of our awkwardness and apprehensions and jumped off the dock toward the shimmering water, when we rose back to the surface with smiles and laughter. Yes, I believe it was in that moment that we ceased being mere bunkmates and companions and became family.

Something similar happens at Baptism. Ritually, men, women and children all go down into the water and rise again transformed. And as one of many rich symbols for baptism, we use the language of family. Undoubtedly, all of God's creatures are loved, but when one is baptized our Prayer Book says that God "adopts us as his children and makes us members of Christ's Body, the Church, and inheritors of the kingdom of God."[1]

Just after the baptisms occur, we will all respond to the newly baptized as one voice saying, "We receive you into the household [or family] of God."

In baptism, a new life begins and a new relationship is forged. We here—like my kin at the state park in Walcott—are as awkward and mismatched a group as any in many ways, but in baptism we go from being relative strangers to loved ones, brothers and sisters in Jesus Christ. And the ties that then bind us deeply are knit in the very heart of God.

In today's Gospel, Jesus talks about the family of God. Some Sadducees approach Jesus with a question about the Resurrection. The Sadducees are suspicious of Jesus and his followers—yet another mismatched group of people, and one who seem to relate to one another at a depth and with a connection the Sadducees cannot understand. The Sadducees don't believe in resurrection. They don't believe in a dimension of life that runs deeper than the life we know. Death is death, and life is subsequently superficial and worldly.

The Sadducees' corrosive cynicism is surely not unfamiliar to us today. We all know those whose philosophy of life is "What you see is what you get." It is a fatalistic outlook, a failure of imagination, and it may be the most popular religion being peddled today. Almost always, it includes a superiority that looks down upon those who have the audacity to hope for new life either in this realm of existence or the next.

With just such condescension, the Sadducees attempt to trip Jesus up with a riddle about a woman who married seven brothers in turn, each of whom subsequently died. If there is resurrection, they ask, in the new life whose wife will she be?

It is a silly scenario and a silly question. They know it, and Jesus knows it. They ask it not because they are interested in Jesus' answer, but in the attempt to make Jesus look foolish. But Jesus will have none of their superficial game; he wants to dive deep. He takes the frame of their question—that of family—and he shifts the conversation to one about new life as children of God. He reveals to the Sadducees that the relationships of those who are transformed by grace have a different character than the relationships of those who live by the ways of the world. Those who enter new life, he says, "are like angels and are children of God."

In his answer, Jesus reveals that in new life our relationships are redefined by a depth unknown to the Sadducees. As children of God, those who enter new life are also brothers and sisters with one another. They bridge the distance the world would set between them. They give up superficiality. They discard their wariness and come together in love. Whatever else resurrection life may mean, it surely means this.

And here's the kicker: The promise that we hold is that the new life does not begin with physical death. Rather, resurrection comes with the dying and rising at baptism, when we go down into the water and emerge in new life.

When one arrived at that campground in Walcott, Arkansas, it was easy to look across the landscape and cynically conclude that what you saw was what you got: an odd and sometimes laughable assortment of mismatched people, a collection of mundane and sometimes tragic lives. But when one chose to stay, and if one decided to don cut-off shorts and plunge into the water, then that first perspective was altogether changed. Where guardedness had been, love emerged. Where virtual strangers had leapt from a dock, family emerged from the water.

So it is here. From an outsider's perspective, those of us who congregate together as the church can surely sometimes seem like an odd and awkward group of people. But just as the state park at Walcott was transformed by the gathered presence of family, so this church becomes the household of God whenever we gather here in love, when we break bread together and share the stories of our faith, and when one of us emerges from the water. We remain the family of God when we depart from this place with love abiding, continuing to regard one another as brothers and sisters in Christ whenever and wherever we meet.

This is the beginning of new life! This is what it means to be children of God! Cynicism cannot corrode this family. The specter of death cannot touch this hope.

Amen.

ENDNOTES

1 *The Book of Common Prayer,* Catechism

Bloody Pond

May 2010 John 5:1-9

After this there was a festival of the Jews, and Jesus went up to Jerusalem.

Now in Jerusalem by the Sheep Gate there is a pool, called in Hebrew Beth-zatha, which has five porticoes. In these lay many invalids—blind, lame, and paralyzed. One man was there who had been ill for thirty-eight years. When Jesus saw him lying there and knew that he had been there a long time, he said to him, 'Do you want to be made well?' The sick man answered him, 'Sir, I have no one to put me into the pool when the water is stirred up; and while I am making my way, someone else steps down ahead of me.' Jesus said to him, 'Stand up, take your mat and walk.' At once the man was made well, and he took up his mat and began to walk. Now that day was a Sabbath.

A week shy of the first anniversary of hostilities between the Northern and Southern states, Confederate General Albert Sidney Johnston launched a surprise attack on the laurel-resting Union army of Ulysses S Grant in southwest Tennessee. No one knew it that April morning, but in some ways the horror of the Civil War would begin that day, and even the horror of all modern warfare. By April 6, 1862, the First Battle of Bull Run had occurred, terrorizing spectators (especially Northern ones), and the epic fight between the ironclad ships *Monitor* and *Merrimac* had ended in stalemate. But no one had any idea what was yet in store.

On April 6, 1862, General Johnston slammed his Army of Mississippi into Grant's Army of the Tennessee. Johnston was killed that first day of battle, and his second-in-command, General Beauregard, failed to pursue the retreating Union army in the night. By morning, General Buell's Army of the Ohio had joined Grant, and the Confederates who had been so close to a game-changing victory the day before were routed.

When the dust settled and the dead were tallied, it was discovered that four thousand men had lost their lives in two days of battle. Another sixteen thousand had been injured—often gruesomely—and many would ultimately die as a result. In 1862 these were staggering statistics; they're staggering today. The Battle of Shiloh was the bloodiest engagement in American history to date, and it still ranks near the top of the list.

I first visited the Shiloh battlefield as a child. I've been back on numerous occasions. Every time I'm drawn to a particular place in the park. Not the "Hornet's Nest" where Union soldiers repulsed repeated Rebel attacks before being overrun; not the peach orchard where blossoms were said to rain down like snow as the shots of rifled muskets riddled the trees. I'm drawn to a tranquil pool nestled among trees that one hundred and fifty-two years ago was given the name "Bloody Pond."

Since the dawn of history until our own day, pools of water have been believed to have healing properties. Hot Springs, Arkansas, has an impressive row of classic bathhouses designed to draw therapeutic water for weary bathers. Warm Springs, Georgia, was developed by FDR in hopes that the mineral waters in the pools there would cure his paralysis.

In John's Gospel, we see such a pool. It is in Jerusalem, and we're told that it is surrounded by five porticoes. Archaeologists have found the remnants of just such a pool—even the porticoes—and so most likely this pool is not the literary fancy of John but rather an actual place sought out for healing. The Gospel tells us that the pool is surrounded by the sick and lame. These wait for the stirring of the water, which to ancient people—even faithful but desperate Jews—was believed to be caused by healing spirits. The infirm then crowd chaotically to the water's edge, pushing and vying for relief from their maladies.

Beginning in the evening of April 6, 1862, horrifically-wounded soldiers in both blue and gray gravitated to the tranquil pool at the edge of the battlefield. As they approached the water, the fight beyond them gave way to different urgency, a desperate hope that the water could soothe them. First vying for space around the pool's crowded edge, soldiers eventually waded or dragged themselves into the water, stirring it up in hopes of healing.

There is a man in our Gospel story who has come to the pool at Jerusalem because of an affliction that has plagued him for thirty-eight years. This is roughly the average lifespan for his day, which is another way for John to tell us that the man experiences his affliction as something that has weighed upon him *forever*. It feels as if it had no beginning and will have no end. It feels, in other words, hopeless.

But the pool offers the man no relief, because others jockey in front of him when the water is stirred, boxing him out and leaving him alone under a portico. Jesus asks the man, "Do you want to be made well?" and the man responds with an honesty that may surprise himself, "Yes," he says in essence, "*but I can't get there on my own.*"

At Bloody Pond on the Shiloh battlefield, no healing was found. The wounds were too severe and deep for cleansing, and with tragic irony the concentration of blood that poured into the water from the wounded rendered it impossible to drink. Not even thirst was slaked as the pond turned thick and murky red and gained its immortal name.

I think I'm drawn to Bloody Pond because of its futility, because of the way it served as a hollow promise that led to death. The waters stirred, but in the stirring they gave not life. They just ran red with blood. Men came there, exerting much effort and their last remaining strength, and they died. After being so wounded they wanted to be made well, but they couldn't get there on their own.

Commentators note that the story we read today in John is unusual in that the paralyzed man's healing is not based upon his faith. Elsewhere, Jesus says to those who've been healed, "Your faith has made you well." But here, after only the man's frank admission that healing is beyond his own power, Jesus says, "Stand up, take your mat and walk." This, then, is the first and greatest step toward a life beyond the painful, aching wounds it may feel as if have plagued us forever, with no beginning and no end in sight.

You see, we are a people who are formed to believe that there is precious little we can't ultimately do for ourselves. Self-sufficiency is, perhaps, our highest virtue. And so, when we are knocked low by life—by physical illness, emotional strain, addiction, moral failing—our first and sometimes persistent response is to seek *on our own* those pools where we can take our cure. We want to wade into them and stir up the water, but there are no miraculous spirits there. We won't find true healing of the human condition on our own. We'll simply churn our blood in futility, and by the time we realize it, we may be too far gone.

Our woundedness is not self-healing. The metaphoric miraculous pools we visit will ultimately disappoint. It is only when we finally say, "I want to be made well, but I can't make it on my own," that healing can begin. That admission— as those in Alcoholics Anonymous have long known with regard to their own disease—allows a different water and a different blood begin to do its work. That admission enables the Son of God to grant standing strength to weakened legs and raise the eyes of heads bowed low.

Healing may not always include *cure*. The alcoholic is always recovering, never recovered; some grief will always rub; some cancers are beyond medicine's reach. But *healing*—that *strength* that comes from beyond us, that *rest* that comes in the arms of the God who loves, that *restoration* that sometimes includes physical cure—can begin when we acknowledge that we are not self-sufficient and when we have the humility to ask for God's help. And healing can be furthered when we accept the assistance of one another, as brothers and sisters called to help each other to the living water's edge.

Then faith will come. Faith is trust and the giving of the heart. It may not burst forth in full bloom like the peach blossoms at Shiloh. But it will grow as we become people who say "I want to be made well, but I can't make it on my own," as we become those who rely not upon futile and deceptive waters but upon the Jesus who gives us the strength to stand up and walk.

Amen.

Darkness

The Valley of the Dry Bones

MARCH 2008   EZEKIEL 37:1-14

The hand of the LORD came upon me, and he brought me out by the spirit of the LORD and set me down in the middle of a valley; it was full of bones. He led me all round them; there were very many lying in the valley, and they were very dry. He said to me, 'Mortal, can these bones live?' I answered, 'O Lord GOD, you know.' Then he said to me, 'Prophesy to these bones, and say to them: O dry bones, hear the word of the LORD. Thus says the Lord GOD to these bones: I will cause breath to enter you, and you shall live. I will lay sinews on you, and will cause flesh to come upon you, and cover you with skin, and put breath in you, and you shall live; and you shall know that I am the LORD.'

So I prophesied as I had been commanded; and as I prophesied, suddenly there was a noise, a rattling, and the bones came together, bone to its bone. I looked, and there were sinews on them, and flesh had come upon them, and skin had covered them; but there was no breath in them. Then he said to me, 'Prophesy to the breath, prophesy, mortal, and say to the breath: Thus says the Lord GOD: Come from the four winds, O breath, and breathe upon these slain, that they may live.' I prophesied as he commanded me, and the breath came into them, and they lived, and stood on their feet, a vast multitude.

Then he said to me, 'Mortal, these bones are the whole house of Israel. They say, "Our bones are dried up, and our hope is lost; we are cut off completely." Therefore prophesy, and say to them, Thus says the Lord GOD: I am going to open your graves, and bring you up from your graves, O my people; and I will bring you back to the land of Israel. And you shall know that I am the LORD, when I open your graves, and bring you up from your graves, O my people. I will put my spirit within you, and you shall live, and I will place you on your own soil; then you shall know that I, the LORD, have spoken and will act, says the LORD.'

I'll never forget the experience. I was seventeen and a student at the Arkansas Governor's School, a six-week college campus summer program in which students enrolled in music, drama, literature, or the social sciences. We spent our days in enlivened classrooms discussing the meaning of life and other topics that never seemed to make their way into the regular curriculum of the Arkansas public schools. As the summer progressed, I came to prefer Governor's School to my real life. The people were interesting, the topics were enlightening, and, if I'm honest, a few of the girls were cute. For those six weeks, we were able to block out the adolescent pressures of the world outside. They ceased to exist, and within the confines of the campus we lived in a kind of utopia, where life was richer and worry-free.

But Governor's School in general is not the experience that I'll remember. Toward the end of the summer, just as I was becoming fully accustomed to the somewhat surreal campus existence that seemed untouched by the world outside, the illusion of my cloistered environment came crashing down. The faculty of Governor's School ushered all the students into the auditorium, and as we light-heartedly settled into our cushioned seats we heard the clickety-clacking whir of a film projector. Without introduction, what began to run on the screen in front of us was the 1955 documentary "Night and Fog."

> *"The hand of the Lord came upon me, and he brought me out by the spirit of the Lord and set me down in the middle of a valley; it was full of bones. He led me all around them; there were very many lying in the valley, and they were very dry. He said to me, 'Mortal, can these bones live?'"*

The documentary "Night and Fog," is thirty-two minutes of the most excruciating footage ever filmed. Released within a decade of the end of World War II, it tells the story of the Auschwitz concentration camp in Poland and the conditions discovered there by the liberating Russian Army in January 1945. The film chronicles the brutality of man against man and the willing ignorance of the cloistered citizens of the Third Reich, under whose noses the Final Solution was carried out. But to my teenage eyes, the images that were unforgettable were of mountainous piles of bodies and bones. I had never before seen such images of the Holocaust. All the sanitized Holocaust photos in my high school textbooks were of Jewish men or women in prison clothes looking forlornly at the camera. But here, bulldozers unceremoniously moved mounds of debris from place to place, and to my horror, the debris was what remained of humanity—broken flesh and sinew—countless lives lost without hope.

In Ezekiel this morning, we witness a vision that provides one of the most provocative passages in all of Scripture. God takes Ezekiel and places him in a wide valley strewn with dry and sun-bleached human bones. These are the bones of the Israelites, who along with Ezekiel himself have been driven from their homes in Judah and cast into exile in a foreign land. Neighbors are separated from neighbors. The familiar languages, locations, aspirations, and dreams are gone. Their lives have been interrupted, and they might as well literally have been scattered like bones, as in Ezekiel's vision. The things of life—the muscles that gave them strength, the sinews that bound them together—have deteriorated to death. The Babylonians who live around them take no notice at all. Their lives are untouched by the misery of the Israelites. For those who benefit from the Empire, life is cloistered from the debris of those who suffer so. Then as now, it is easy to be willfully ignorant of those who live without hope.

The Valley of the Dry Bones exists wherever hope is lost and lives are interrupted, wherever visions of life have gone unrealized, wherever anxiety stifles joy. Human history is, in many respects, the history of this Valley, an endless account of individuals and communities who have found themselves scattered like dry and sun-bleached bone.

And we equally find the Valley of the Dry Bones in our own time. Those trapped in it, without strength or hope, exist in places like Sudan and Myanmar...but also on the streets of our own desperate inner cities. And in our manicured suburbs. And in the very pews of the church.

Have you seen the Valley of the Dry Bones? Has your life been interrupted by illness or depression, by circumstances that seemed to happen to you despite your best efforts? Have your muscles lost their strength and the sinews that connect you meaningfully to the world around you deteriorated?

Indeed, in the church we see evidence of the Valley every day. Through the fine doors of our impressive edifices walk those whose lives have descended into the Valley of the Dry Bones. Some are our own parishioners and others are not. Some are ill or have loved ones who are ill. Some suffer addictions. Some have lost jobs and can't purchase heating oil. Others, for reasons they can't identify, experience uncertainty or fear, or, try as they might, cannot feel anything at all. All have suffered pain and loss and seek hope where hope is gone.

Do we take notice? As a teenager at Governor's School I was lulled into a cloistered existence, and it was only the shock of "Night and Fog" that rattled me into recognizing the depths of hopelessness and despair that exist in the world. And for the German people themselves in the 1930s and 40s, economic and military security was enough to make them cloister themselves and shield their eyes against the dry bones scattered all around them.

In the church, we can easily come and go, kneeling in stunning places of worship, and giving thanks to God for our own lives, taking no notice of those among us who live without hope. We can do that, until such time that we each find ourselves falling into the Valley of the Dry Bones, needing someone to offer us hope where hope is gone.

Or, we can live differently. Ezekiel gives us the model. When his people are thrust into the Valley, he goes with them. He does not render himself willfully ignorant of their plight. And when he finds them hopeless, Ezekiel listens for a word to share with them. God shows Ezekiel the Valley so that he may offer the dry bones of his people God's promise. Through Ezekiel, the Lord says to the Israelites, "I am going to open your graves, and bring you up from your graves, O my people...And you shall know that I am the Lord...I will put my spirit within you, and you shall live."

God promises to put bone upon bone, to give hope to those without hope and breathe into them new life. And yet, for those who have suffered and are without hope, even such a promise is difficult to embrace. Even after God has begun this work, and muscle has grown upon bone, the people cry, "Our bones are dried up, and our hope is lost!" Only because Ezekiel stays with them—because he embodies in his person the love that God promises—encouraging and reminding the Israelites of God's vision of life that replaces the Valley of the Dry Bones, are the people able to breathe the breath of God.

Wendell Berry describes our salvation as "that precarious interplay of effort and grace."[1] The effort comes from those of us who go down into the Valley to lift one another up, knowing that someday we will be trapped in the Valley and have desperate need of our brothers and sisters. The grace comes from God alone whose word we share. As Lent moves toward Holy Week, our focus will hone in on the One who forever moves into the Valley of the Dry Bones on our behalf, who goes down into the graves of our lives to breathe resurrection into us. We are given this year the blessed opportunity to go there with him, to be for one another in the Valley of the Dry Bones the agent of God who says, "I will bring you up from your graves. I will put my spirit within you, and you shall live."

Amen.

ENDNOTE

1 Wendell Berry, *That Distant Land* (Washington, DC: Counterpoint Press, 2012), 123.

Hell

JULY 2008   MATTHEW 13:24-30, 34-36

He put before them another parable: 'The kingdom of heaven may be compared to someone who sowed good seed in his field; but while everybody was asleep, an enemy came and sowed weeds among the wheat, and then went away. So when the plants came up and bore grain, then the weeds appeared as well. And the slaves of the householder came and said to him, "Master, did you not sow good seed in your field? Where, then, did these weeds come from?" He answered, "An enemy has done this." The slaves said to him, "Then do you want us to go and gather them?" But he replied, "No; for in gathering the weeds you would uproot the wheat along with them. Let both of them grow together until the harvest; and at harvest time I will tell the reapers, Collect the weeds first and bind them in bundles to be burned, but gather the wheat into my barn."'

Then he left the crowds and went into the house. And his disciples approached him, saying, 'Explain to us the parable of the weeds of the field.' He answered, 'The one who sows the good seed is the Son of Man; the field is the world, and the good seed are the children of the kingdom; the weeds are the children of the evil one, and the enemy who sowed them is the devil; the harvest is the end of the age, and the reapers are angels. Just as the weeds are collected and burned up with fire, so will it be at the end of the age. The Son of Man will send his angels, and they will collect out of his kingdom all causes of sin and all evildoers, and they will throw them into the furnace of fire, where there will be weeping and gnashing of teeth. Then the righteous will shine like the sun in the kingdom of their Father. Let anyone with ears listen!

There are passages of Scripture upon which Episcopal priests love to preach. This Gospel passage is not one of them! This passage speaks of wheat and weeds—or "tares," as is the more traditional rendering. The tares symbolize the "children of the evil one," and Jesus says at harvest time they will be sifted from the wheat and thrown into the fire where there will be "weeping and gnashing of teeth." This image seems far removed from the gentle and embracing Christ whom the Episcopal Church does such a commendable job communicating to the world.

Episcopal priests don't like to preach on passages like this one. But we must. Otherwise we practice buffet Christianity, in which we pick and choose to pay attention to the things in our faith that make us comfortable while ignoring all the rest. In that case, our faith becomes a palliative, a creamy drink on a cold night that warms us inside and helps us to sleep. Faith is, at times, surely that. But it is not only that. Our God of tenderness and love is also a God whose love lays claim to us. Our God is one who requires, for our wholeness and good, that we pursue holiness and give up destructive ways of living. And if we don't, there are consequences. Even Episcopal priests must, on rare occasion, speak of hell.

The prevailing cultural image of hell is colored perhaps by no one so much as Dante, the fourteenth century poet in whose epic poem *The Inferno* is inscribed above the gates of hell, "Abandon all hope, ye who enter here." Within hell, the souls of the sinful are punished, burned in flame, gnawed at by demons and the devil himself. Most importantly, all punishment in hell is punitive. In other words, its purpose is to apply endless suffering as retribution for sin.

This is the idea of hell most of us readily recognize. As a consequence, some of us fear hell as a place to be avoided while others reject the idea as abhorrent, disbelieving that God could ever punish his children in such a place, even as a consequence of their own fault.

What to do with the idea of hell? Well, one group has figured out the answer. Moviemakers in Hollywood have for forty years riffed on Dante's and similar illustrations. In recent years, the movies *Hellboy* and *Hellboy II* were huge box office money-makers. But what about the rest of us? What do we do with hell?

In order to consider that question, we need to look with care at today's parable. Most likely, the disciples have come to Jesus with a concern that there are some among them with ulterior motives. There are sinners among the saved, to put it one way. The disciples ask Jesus, "Should we seek to identify the bad seeds and get rid of them? Should we weed them out?"

Jesus knows his disciples are not equipped to discern who among them is wheat and who is weed. So he shares a parable about a farmer whose wheat field is riddled with tares. Tares are a weed that resembles wheat so closely that even a careful eye has trouble telling the difference. On the one hand, if one attempts to pull out the tares, he will invariably pull out much good wheat by mistake, and on the other, many tares themselves will remain unnoticed. Weeding can be destructive when one is not sure of the difference between the good and the bad.

We know this to be true in our context as well. In business, in social settings, and in love we have difficulty discerning who is pure and who operates with only a superficial veil of goodness behind which lies all manner of self-serving motives. And when we do discern, one of the tragedies of life is that we're often wrong. We trust those we shouldn't (often with disastrous consequences), and we accuse those who we later find to have wanted only the best for us. It is difficult for us to separate the wheat from the tares. It is difficult for us to know who to embrace and who to condemn.

Yet the sifting will occur, Jesus assures his followers. It will be accomplished at the end of time. Then, there will be no disguise. Those who now hide cruelty behind a mask of kindness will be exposed, and what awaits them is the "furnace of fire."

This should be good news, right? I mean, we sit here in the house of God, worshiping Christ on bended knees as his followers. We are surely among the children of the kingdom, destined for light. It is those who wrong us, who pretend to befriend us only to do us harm, who will be cast into darkness.

It should be good news, but it doesn't feel that way, because we have a foreboding sense that the intermingling of wheat and weeds is more complicated than that.

We know in our lives—I know in my life—that within each of us there is good and bad. Even after becoming part of the family of God, we sometimes embrace one another with one arm and stab in the back with the other. We act out of anger, resentment, pettiness, and pride. By God's grace we are capable of love, and as we grow in Christ that capacity, we pray, increases by leaps and bounds. But we know that within each and every one of us there is wheat and there is tare. It's not simply a matter of good people and bad people. It is, rather, a matter of the good and bad that resides in me...and in you.

This makes the notion of hell a bit trickier, doesn't it? Who, exactly, gets cast into the fire? Some solve this conundrum with the language of "once saved, always saved," claiming that a singular conversion experience serves to punch one's ticket at the end of time. On one level, they're right. God's promise of ultimate salvation for those who live in Christ is unwavering. But their solution doesn't do justice, it seems to me, to the complexity of Jesus' parable. Jesus says that, ultimately, "all causes of sin" will be cast into the fire, and even in the lives of those committed to Christ often the causes of sin still prevail.

Our tradition offers us other images of hell that may be helpful. One more ancient and mostly neglected vision is that of the great Church father St. Gregory of Nyssa. For Dante, you'll recall that hell was punitive. It was retribution for sin. Gregory, though, views hell very differently. Just as God's whole plan of salvation intends to restore and reconcile us to God, Gregory says, even hell itself intends to restore us.

Gregory agrees that wheat and tare exist in each of us.[1] Even those of us who have opened our lives to Christ continue to live with all the mixed motives I articulated earlier. To describe our lives Gregory uses the image of a precious metal amalgamated with baser ones. We have gold in us, but we are also riddled with rust and lead. Yet, God wants to embrace us fully. His love is pure. God wants so to infuse us with his light and love that the gold in us shines, but the tarnish that is also within us can't abide in God's presence anymore than a shadow can remain when the sun fills its corner. The God who saves us, who claims us as his own, also desires wholeness for us. And wholeness—ultimate and full reconciliation with our brothers and sisters and with our God—requires that these things be burned away. Pure love leaves no room for hatred, for pettiness, for selfishness, or for pride. And so, in Gregory's image, hell is that fire which burns away our rust and ruin. He borrows language from the Old Testament prophet Malachi and calls hell a refiner's fire that restores our souls to their original God-given luster.

Hell, then, becomes something far different than the notion we've inherited from Dante. It becomes, paradoxically, a place of hope rather than hopelessness. It becomes not a pit of despair but a tool in God's economy of salvation. It becomes the place where, as Jesus says today, "all causes of sin" are burned away and one comes out on the other side able to live and love purely, able to accept the embrace of the God of love.

For many, the melting away of those dark and destructive parts of us happens in this life. But is the experience always one of hell? No. It may occur as gently as snow melts from thawing landscape, as we willingly and through grace give up our old lives. But it may not. I once spoke to a recovering alcoholic whose life previously had been defined by his addiction. He knew when and where he'd experienced hell. Drinking itself, he told me, he had not experienced as hell. On many levels it was the life he'd have chosen to continue living, leaving an ever longer trail of destruction in his wake. But neither his community nor his God would allow him to remain in such darkness. "They put me through hell," he told me, and he meant it. He experienced hell in the excruciating and painful process of giving up alcohol and repairing the relationships he'd so disastrously damaged. Gregory of Nyssa's idea of hell made perfect sense to him.

The addict is perhaps the extreme example. But there are countless others who experience in this life the excruciating yet purifying refiner's fire that comes with having burned away by the power of Christ and the community the destructive and harmful things that have defined us: our anger, our resentments, our pettiness, and our pride. It is a passage through hell giving these things up, but on the other side is light.

The reality still remains, as Jesus says, that there will be those who will cling to these things throughout life. At the end of time, then, there will be a reckoning. In other words, Gregory believes that for some hell is a real, metaphysical place. But even then the reason is not vengeance but love. God seeks not retribution but restoration, the removal of those things that separate us from our Creator. And even hell then, hopes Gregory, has at its far side our wholeness and embrace by God.

And so, we actually come full circle. This sermon has been, after all, one of good news. St. Gregory's vision of hell is only one among many, but it is one I find compelling. For Gregory, the defining characteristic of hell is that it seeks to burn, to dispel from us the destructive parts of who we are and strengthen in us the power of love. Such hell is painful, because it's always painful to let go of the things by which we've defined ourselves, no matter how destructive they may be. But on hell's other side we find the God of love in whom we can then live fully, who invites us into his kingdom to shine like the sun as children of light.

Amen.

Endnotes

1 This exposition is drawn from Gregory of Nyssa's *Great Catechism*, chapter XXVI.

Coal Dust

London doesn't have fog to speak of. That's surprising, isn't it? One of the most ubiquitous Victorian images in literature and film is of London streets shrouded in a thick and menacing fog the color of pea soup. The world's most successful raincoat company—an American company, by the way—built its empire on the very name "London Fog." And yet, the truth is that London has no fog to speak of.

This seeming puzzle is easily solved when we realize that the fog of Victorian London was never of the meteorological variety. It was actually smog caused by millions of coal-fired home furnaces, each spitting out yellowish black dust into the atmosphere. The fog was really coal dust.[1]

When I moved to Roanoke, Virginia, people attempted to orient me to my new home with reference to the river. "The church is north of the river," they'd say, or "Black Dog Salvage is next to Memorial Bridge over the river." I moved here from Memphis, Tennessee. The river of my imagination is the Mighty Mississippi, of thunderous power and half a mile wide. I drove around this town for weeks before I realized the "river" to which people referred was that creek that runs alongside the soccer fields!

But I hadn't been in Roanoke long before a different landmark did strike me with awe comparable to that of the Mississippi River. I would drive down Jefferson Street and over the overpass in front of Roanoke Memorial Hospital, and I would see below burgeoning coal cars on the railroad tracks stretching as far as the eye can see. Everyday. Do you realize how remarkable a sight that is? The trains carry their endless cargo from West Virginia to Norfolk, from which point the coal is shipped and powers cities and towns all over the world, including—somewhat ironically—cities and towns in England.

For decades, homes and businesses in Roanoke were heated by coal-fired furnaces, each of which poured coal dust into our atmosphere. In addition, the relentless caravan of coal-fired trains that thundered through town spewed soot of their own. Like London, Roanoke's air could be thick with coal dust, and it settled everywhere. Older parishioners will tell you they recall the endless chore of dusting black embers and coal grit from their window sills. Ash and dust trapped high in the stratosphere would fall from the sky in rain, and when the water evaporated, the coal dust was left to sift through roofs and into attics, to lie there unnoticed perhaps forever.[2]

When we were restoring the St. John's Church the time came to remove the ceiling so that wiring could be replaced and insulation added. When the workmen began to pull down the slats, they were immediately covered by a thick layer of ancient coal dust that had been trapped in our ceiling for years. It instantly wafted down and filled the air, turning the nave into a miniature of Victorian London. To walk through the space was to move through a haze of dust and ash, and I thought, "Remember that you are dust, and to dust you shall return."

For a few days after that, I was drawn from my office to the church almost compulsively. The dust lingered, and it was mesmerizing. It symbolized for me all the things that holy building has seen, all the changes to which it has stood silent witness, as generations of people have been born, grown old, and died over more than a century. The dust also symbolized all those people who have walked down the church's aisles, who have prayed there, and worried, and cried, and laughed. That dust was the stuff of old verger and sexton Norman Taylor—buried in his verger's robes—who was sometimes called out in the middle of the frigid night to re-stoke St. John's own coal-fired furnace when it had gone out. It was the stuff of the Rev. Richard Beasley, beloved rector whose portrait I passed by every day in the hall, who stepped down from this pulpit on a cold October Sunday morning and minutes later collapsed and died in the arms of his friend, Dr. Bob Bondurant. It was the stuff of the scores of people buried here, lives with stories each, who have ranged in age from seventeen months to ninety-seven years.

We have a lot in common with coal. We are coal, for the most part, simply carbon less-compressed and with a lot of protein and water mixed in. Eventually we will become the coal dust raining down onto someone else's roof, collecting in someone else's attic.

It is that of which Ash Wednesday reminds us. We are but dust. We will become the mesmerizing cloud through which others walk and wonder about the lives our dust symbolizes, the lives we lived. They will travel through the gauzy cloud of memory and strive to know what mattered to us and why and how we held it dear, so that we can form them just as we are formed by those who have gone before. We're only here for a little while. What we do now, what we say now, how we love now—or fail to love—matters, and it matters in ways that will long outlast us.

On my third trip down to the church to walk through the haze of ashes, it was early morning on a sunny day. Through the cloud I could see ahead of me a soft glow of light. I walked through the church—through the cloud—and up onto the chancel, where I could finally and only then see that what had appeared as a faint glow was, in fact, blazing sunlight shining through the empty tomb of our Resurrection window above the high altar.

When the weight of ashes hangs heavy on us this Lent, we must also remember that image. There is the promise that our lives lived here are a foretaste, a prelude to life abundant in the fullness of God. That promise is real. The alleluias we will sing come Easter Day touch the heart of a real God in whom nothing is lost. But we can only get there through here. Before Easter comes Lent, and we can only recognize the shining sun if we approach it through the cloud of ashes.

And so, thinking back over those generations of folk whom the coal dust symbolizes we ask: Both literally and figuratively, to whom do we provide warmth in the cold night? What furnaces do we stoke? What message do we preach? What friend do we embrace? Soon enough we will be but ashes. What story will our ashes tell?

Amen.

ENDNOTES

1 "Pea soup fog," *Wikipedia: The Free Encyclopedia*, https://en.wikipedia.org/wiki/Pea_soup_fog (accessed November 17, 2013).

2 I owe these details of past life in Roanoke to the professional expertise and recollections of Mary Field Green, chair of the St. John's Episcopal Church Archives and Earle Shumate, parishioner and architect.

Good Friday

APRIL 2010   MARK 15:25-39

It was nine o'clock in the morning when they crucified him. The inscription of the charge against him read, 'The King of the Jews.' And with him they crucified two bandits, one on his right and one on his left. Those who passed by derided him, shaking their heads and saying, 'Aha! You who would destroy the temple and build it in three days, save yourself, and come down from the cross!' In the same way the chief priests, along with the scribes, were also mocking him among themselves and saying, 'He saved others; he cannot save himself. Let the Messiah, the King of Israel, come down from the cross now, so that we may see and believe.' Those who were crucified with him also taunted him.

When it was noon, darkness came over the whole land until three in the afternoon. At three o'clock Jesus cried out with a loud voice, 'Eloi, Eloi, lema sabachthani?' which means, 'My God, my God, why have you forsaken me?' When some of the bystanders heard it, they said, 'Listen, he is calling for Elijah.' And someone ran, filled a sponge with sour wine, put it on a stick, and gave it to him to drink, saying, 'Wait, let us see whether Elijah will come to take him down.' Then Jesus gave a loud cry and breathed his last. And the curtain of the temple was torn in two, from top to bottom. Now when the centurion, who stood facing him, saw that in this way he breathed his last, he said, 'Truly this man was God's Son!'

At nine o'clock this morning, the Son of God was hung on the cross. His hands and feet were nailed, tender flesh pierced by the hard weight of a hammer. He was raised unceremoniously into the air, jarred as the cross slammed into its base, and immediately found it difficult to breathe as the torture of crucifixion did its work asphyxiating him.

Why? Why do words of salvation spark murderous fervor in men? Why did some find themselves compelled to plot and scheme, and when the game was afoot, why did trusted friends flee? Why, at three o'clock, when Jesus himself realized his final moments were at hand, did he who had always felt the most intimate proximity to God experience God's utter absence, crying to his Abba, "My God, my God, why have you forsaken me?"

These are the questions suggested by the story, but in truth they are universal questions. If we believe, as we say we do, that in Jesus God was pleased to dwell, and if we believe, as we say we do, that God is equally incarnate in the world round about us, then why, as Josiah Royce asks, "is there so much evil in [the world]—so much darkness, ignorance, misery, disappointment, warfare, hatred, disease [and] death?"[1]

Why do earthquakes destroy whole cities? Why do people everywhere react and respond to one another with suspicion and fear, whether religious, racial, or economic? Why do parents neglect and abuse their children unto death? Why do age, addiction, and disease ravage those we love? Why does life not turn out as we plan? Why does it seem that God has forsaken us? It is enough to make one rail at God. So much darkness, ignorance, misery, disappointment, and death.

Long before *Titanic*, there was *The Poseidon Adventure*, a movie made from the best-selling novel, and one that has held up surprisingly well over the years. In the midst of a frolicking New Year's Eve party, the luxury cruise liner Poseidon is capsized by a tidal wave, and the scene of celebration becomes a tomb floating upside down on the sea, as quickly as we shifted from joy to solemnity on Palm Sunday. Most passengers die in the initial onslaught, but a small and misfit band struggles to find a way out to the light of day. Eventually they make it almost to the stern where they hope they can escape when a pipe bursts, blocking their way with a jet of scalding steam. The valve wheel to shut off the steam—the group's salvation, in other words—is across a chasm beneath which is an abyss of fire and water. Whoever leaps across to the wheel will be scalded and will not be able to jump back.

Frank Scott, a minister played by Gene Hackman, looks through the deadly steam and across at the valve wheel and screams at God, "What more do you want of us? We've come all this way, no thanks to you…we didn't ask you to fight for us, but don't fight against us! Leave us alone! How many more sacrifices? How much more blood? How many more lives?"

Forsaken by God, Scott leaps across the chasm to the valve wheel and barely grabs hold of it. Scorching steam envelopes him, and with painstaking slowness, hand-over-hand, he closes the valve. The steam dissipates, and a burned and wasted Rev. Scott turns around to face his companions across the chasm. "Now you can make it!" he yells to them, "Keep going!" With his strength spent, Scott lets go of the wheel and drops to his death in fire and water.

Good Friday leads to despair if sacrifice is the end, because despair is, as Victor Frankl offered, suffering without meaning.[2] If Jesus' crucifixion is merely emblematic of the world's horror—if it's just a reminder that human beings always ultimately destroy what is good—then God has forsaken us, and we should despair.

But remember what sets Christians apart from others. We attest… we believe… we give our hearts to the affirmation that the man on the cross is also God. He hangs there because God is incarnate in all things. Jesus is pierced, he struggles for breath, he experiences the forsakenness of his Abba so to be incarnate even in our pain, to be present even in our suffering.

The same Josiah Royce who earlier asked about the darkness in our world answers his own question by saying that, in Jesus, God "descends into our lives, and scalded with our pain" becomes *grafted* to us in our pain. With us in our suffering God is loyal, God endures, God loves.

Jesus' suffering is not despair. Its meaning is to join him with us in our own suffering.

Our suffering is not despair, because God-in-Christ is in the midst of it with us. Painstakingly, he turns the valve wheel and reduces the scalding steam. He leaps across the chasms when we are not able, and he turns to us and says, "I am with you. Now you can make it. Keep going."

This church in which we worship is also called a "nave." That is a nautical term, and the church is designed so that the ceiling resembles the underbelly of an overturned ship. Except this ship is only tomb today and tomorrow. On Sunday the tomb will be empty, the church will be transformed, and we will see the light of day. For now, let us thank God that Jesus bears the cross—bears our crosses—so we don't have to do so alone.

Amen.

ENDNOTES

1 John Clendenning, *The Life and Thought of Josiah Royce* (Nashville: Vanderbilt University Press, 1999), 334.

2 Victor Frankl, *Contribution to Spirituality and Aging*, ed. Melvin A. Kimble (New York: The Hawthorne Pastoral Press, 2000), 60.

The Death of Osama Bin Laden

MAY 2011

LUKE 24:13-35

Now on that same day two of them were going to a village called Emmaus, about seven miles from Jerusalem, and talking with each other about all these things that had happened. While they were talking and discussing, Jesus himself came near and went with them, but their eyes were kept from recognizing him. And he said to them, 'What are you discussing with each other while you walk along?' They stood still, looking sad. Then one of them, whose name was Cleopas, answered him, 'Are you the only stranger in Jerusalem who does not know the things that have taken place there in these days?' He asked them, 'What things?' They replied, 'The things about Jesus of Nazareth, who was a prophet mighty in deed and word before God and all the people, and how our chief priests and leaders handed him over to be condemned to death and crucified him. But we had hoped that he was the one to redeem Israel. Yes, and besides all this, it is now the third day since these things took place. Moreover, some women of our group astounded us. They were at the tomb early this morning, and when they did not find his body there, they came back and told us that they had indeed seen a vision of angels who said that he was alive. Some of those who were with us went to the tomb and found it just as the women had said; but they did not see him.' Then he said to them, 'Oh, how foolish you are, and how slow of heart to believe all that the prophets have declared! Was it not necessary that the Messiah should suffer these things and then enter into his glory?' Then beginning with Moses and all the prophets, he interpreted to them the things about himself in all the scriptures.

As they came near the village to which they were going, he walked ahead as if he were going on. But they urged him strongly, saying, 'Stay with us, because it is almost evening and the day is now nearly over.' So he went in to stay with them. When he was at the table with them, he took bread, blessed and broke it, and gave it to them. Then their eyes were opened, and they recognized him; and he vanished from their sight. They said to each other, 'Were not our hearts burning within us while he was talking to us on the road, while he was opening the scriptures to us?' That same hour they got up and returned to Jerusalem; and they found the eleven and their companions gathered together. They were saying, 'The Lord has risen indeed, and he has appeared to Simon!' Then they told what had happened on the road, and how he had been made known to them in the breaking of the bread.

The first thing you notice is the whiteness of the nurse's uniform. Against the grey of the background, it's as vivid as fresh cotton. Her back is arched, and the small of it rests on the strong and broad hand of a sailor. She balances delicately on one leg, with the other kicked back at a forty-five degree angle. Her arm dangles at her side, revealing that it is the sailor's strength and not any effort of her own that keeps her standing. With one arm he holds her back, and with the other he cradles her neck. His cap is pushed back on his head, and he leans into her with passion.

We can't see either of their faces, because they are engaged in the most famous kiss of the 20th century. It is a celebratory kiss. We know this because of the ticker tape on the pavement and the expressions on the faces of those in the background. All are cheering and smiling. In a sense, everyone in the scene is taking part in that kiss.

The date is August 14, 1945, Victory over Japan Day, when the Empire of Japan signaled its surrender to ultimately, finally, totally end the Second World War. When the war ended, people celebrated.

This past week people again celebrated. Spontaneous parties erupted outside the White House. On college campuses, people gathered in joyous abandon.

The descriptor repeatedly used in the newspaper was "euphoria" at the death of Osama bin Laden.

In a few months we'll commemorate the tenth anniversary of September 11, 2001. That day affected me as much as it did many, though I'm sure less than some. I had no close personal friends in the Twin Towers that day. But I did know Sara Low, one of the flight attendants on American Airlines Flight 11 which collided with the North Tower. She was the sister of a college friend. I'd met her several times.

My college roommate had only just moved to Washington, D.C. a few weeks before the attack. It was Chris who called me early that morning as I was walking out the door to a seminary class and told me to turn on the television, just in time to see the second plane make impact. After the Pentagon was hit, Chris and I lost telephone contact, and I worried for him throughout that day and the next, until we were able to reconnect.

At the Church of the Holy Apostles in Collierville, Tennessee, I had a couple in the parish who had previously worked for a New York accounting firm based in the World Trade Center. Many of their friends and colleagues were killed on 9/11.

That was all a decade ago. In the interim our country has fought two wars. As a nation, we are conflicted over the motives for one of those wars and over the long lack of priority given the other. As a community, we pray for those we know and love who serve in uniform in harm's way even this very day. On doubting days we wonder if, and on sure days we believe, our expense of emotion and blood is making the United States safer in the world.

This decade-long burden we still bore on Sunday last, when the President of the United States interrupted our television viewing to tell us that Osama bin Laden had been killed. In the succeeding days, we have learned the stunning precision with which the Navy SEAL operation was carried out. In the process of eliminating Osama bin Laden, none of our soldiers and only one enemy noncombatant were killed.

As Christian people, how should we feel about such things, first about the execution and second about the subsequent celebrations? Undoubtedly, some cringe at broaching the topic at all. It seems dangerously close to mixing religion and politics. And yet, the saints of the Church have always asked such questions: Augustine, Martin Luther, Karl Barth, Martin Luther King, Jr. Jesus himself asked such questions. If our faith is to be more than merely a Sunday lozenge that soothes our scratchy souls, it must bear upon the way we walk through the world. And so, the questions must be asked and answers must be attempted.

Our first instinct will be to answer them through our emotional lenses, our need for closure, and our fear of an enemy who lurks in shadow. That instinct is natural and human, but we must in humility acknowledge that it is not *Christian*. In today's Gospel reading—the Walk to Emmaus, which we read on the Third Sunday of Easter—we find two disciples of Jesus who are also at an emotional pitch. Their teacher has been killed, but now his body has disappeared, denying them closure. They fear the powers who killed him. They share these concerns with the stranger who walks with them on the road, but they remain so confused that they don't recognize who he is or what he tells them in return. Only when he sits with them and enacts Eucharist—taking bread, blessing it, breaking it, and giving it to them—are their eyes opened. Only then do they recognize the stranger as Jesus and understand his teaching.

This is a crucial point for us, and this is what it means: The bread symbolizes Jesus himself. He is broken for us, and only with our eyes open to that sacrifice can we understand how we are to respond to events in the world. Apart from the Gospel of Jesus, we are bound to respond wrongly.

First, the execution of bin Laden itself. St. Paul tells us in the 13th chapter of Romans that the governing authority is the agent of God "to execute wrath on the wrongdoer."

Perhaps no Christian has wrestled with what this means so much as Martin Luther. Luther said if we lived in a world where everyone followed the teaching of Jesus—where everyone lived as a Christian rather than merely claiming to be Christian—we'd have no need for authority that bears a sword. But we do not live in such a world. We live in a world in which the power of evil causes people, in Luther's words, to "devour one another." In such a world, we must live with the paradox that sometimes the sword is necessary "to bring about peace and prevent evil deeds."

Martin Luther believed that no Christian should take up the sword in self-defense, but "*for another* he can and ought to wield [the sword] and invoke it, so that wickedness may be hindered"[1] and "evil and injustice"[2] punished.

In other words, to end what we rightly can call the evil work of Osama bin Laden, which not only led to the deaths of three thousand American civilians a decade ago but also the deaths of thousands more people across the globe over the years, we can say that the execution of bin Laden was just, and perhaps even faithful.

But what of the celebrations? They strike me as different in kind to those celebrations in Times Square and elsewhere at the end of World War II. Those events, both spontaneous and planned, were in essence celebrations of life. In other words, no one cheered the dropping of the bomb on Hiroshima. Rather, what caused the euphoria in those days was the realization that no more lives would be lost, either ours of those of our enemies. War was ending. Light had overcome darkness.

This week, though, the celebrations have been focused not upon the end of a conflict or the saving of lives (although we can hope that both of these may ultimately result from last Sunday's event). The celebrations have focused upon the fact of a man's death. An enemy's death and a necessary death to be sure, but a death all the same. And the wild abandon, the chanting and slogans, have seemed more apt for the ending of a football game. What would be the Christian argument against such celebration in this case?

There is an ancient Jewish midrash that says when the Israelites escaped the Red Sea, and the sea collapsed on the Egyptians drowning them, the angels in heaven began to rejoice. They looked over at God, who sat in stony silence. Finally, God rebuked them with his tears saying, "These, too, were my children."

Elsewhere God says through the prophet Ezekiel, "I take no pleasure in the death of the wicked, but would rather they turn from their ways and live."[3]

In addition to commanding us to love our enemies, Jesus himself grieved for those who butchered him (Can you imagine?), begging God's forgiveness for the very men who nailed him to the cross, trading his own brokenness for the brokenness of the world in order to save it.

The death of any of God's children is cause for grief, especially when that death comes as the inevitable end of a life spent destroying other of God's beloved children, as the end of a wasted life.

Two weeks ago I stood at the base of the Washington Monument. To my right was the Capitol Building. In front of me was the White House. Two my left was the Lincoln Memorial. And at my side were my children. It was awesome. Never was I more grateful to be an American citizen. As an American, I am relieved that Osama bin Laden is dead. Most likely people will live because he no longer does. Perhaps Americans will come home sooner because he is gone.

As a Christian, I will not whoop and cheer his death. I will—I hope we will—pray for this world in which men devour one another; pray for this world in which the sword is a necessary instrument of peace; pray that the authorities God grants the right to wield that sword use it with wisdom and justice; and pray for that day to end all days, when swords are unnecessary, terror unknown, and the love of God reigns in all people. Amen.

Amen.

ENDNOTES

1 Martin Luther, *Martin Luther, Selections From His Writings*, ed. John Dillenberger (New York: Doubleday, 1962), 381.

2 Ibid., 375.

3 Ezekiel 18:23.

Light

The Star
In Our Eyes

JANUARY 2008   MATTHEW 2:1-12

*In the time of King Herod, after Jesus was born in Bethlehem of Judea, wise men
from the East came to Jerusalem, asking, "Where is the child who has been born
king of the Jews? For we observed his star at its rising, and have come to pay him
homage." When King Herod heard this, he was frightened, and all Jerusalem with
him; and calling together all the chief priests and scribes of the people, he inquired
of them where the Messiah was to be born. They told him, "In Bethlehem of Judea;
for so it has been written by the prophet: 'And you, Bethlehem, in the land of Judah,
are by no means least among the rulers of Judah; for from you shall come a ruler who
is to shepherd my people Israel.'" Then Herod secretly called for the wise men and
learned from them the exact time when the star had appeared. Then he sent them to
Bethlehem, saying, "Go and search diligently for the child; and when you have found
him, bring me word so that I may also go and pay him homage."*

*When they had heard the king, they set out; and there, ahead of them, went the star
that they had seen at its rising, until it stopped over the place where the child was.
When they saw that the star had stopped, they were overwhelmed with joy.   On
entering the house, they saw the child with Mary his mother; and they knelt down
and paid him homage. Then, opening their treasure chests, they offered him gifts of
gold, frankincense, and myrrh.   And having been warned in a dream not to return
to Herod, they left for their own country by another road.*

My mother will tell you that the greatest gift she ever received was a tin of Vienna sausages. You all know Vienna sausages: mini-hot dogs dunked in a briny, jelly-like liquid and sealed in a half-sized aluminum can with a peal-back top. Vienna sausages are not what one would normally think of as the gift to top all gifts. But this particular gift came from my three-year-old younger brother, the first year that my grandfather had given him Christmas money of his own with which to purchase gifts for those he most loved. And there was no one my brother loved more than our mom; she put stars in his eyes. On our shopping expedition, my brother paced the aisles of Wal-Mart trying to determine the most exalted gift to explain to our mother and to all those around just how much he loved and cherished her. And then, in the canned meats aisle, he found it. As though haloed at eye-level in front of him like, well, an epiphany, there were the Vienna sausages. My brother ate them several times a week; to him they were like little links of jelly-drenched heaven. And so, with the blissful ignorance of a three-year-old who has never heard of Upton Sinclair and has no idea in what a Vienna sausage actually consists, his tiny little fingers grabbed a can off the shelf to take home to my mother, the center of his world and the love of his life. I'd harbor a guess that each mother in this room would have opened that tin of sausages on Christmas Day and agreed that it was the greatest gift she'd ever received.

The beginning of Matthew's second chapter is another story of gifts. On the day of Epiphany, which actually rarely falls on a Sunday, we read the rather mysterious account of three men in the East who find a star in their own eyes. Matthew doesn't tell from where these three come. In his parlance, "the East" intends to signify somewhere different and far away. These aren't from close by, in other words. Wherever it is from which they begin, a sign appears in the heavens, and the three feel compelled to follow it. The star leads them to Judea, where they consult with Herod the king. The three then continue on to Bethlehem, where the star in the heavens stops over the humble house sheltering a small child with his mother. "Little one," they say, "it is you who put the star in *our* eyes. We bring you gifts."

What the three then present may sound as strange to us as a tin of Vienna sausages. The wise men give the child gold, frankincense, and myrrh. The heart of this Epiphany story, like the story I shared of my brother's gift to my mother, is that the particular gifts of the wise men have meaning far beyond what we, on the surface, can discern. The word "epiphany" means "revealing," and in their choice of gifts the strange men from the East reveal to us just who this child is to them.

Gold is not a gift that one gives to a baby. But it *is* a gift that one presents to a king.

Frankincense—that sweet-smelling incense that is burned even to this day in thuribles before altars in churches just like this one—is a gift given to a priest.

And Myrrh is an anointing oil, a solemn gift given to a prophet, signifying that he is anointed to speak God's word. It is also the oil for anointing the dead, signifying that the prophet is also almost assuredly the target of those who would deny God's word.

King, priest, prophet. When the three men look at the child Jesus, this is what they see. Other than perhaps Mary herself, I suspect that few present in Bethlehem call them wise. Those who are closest to the little family look at the ragged child and his young, ragged parents—outsiders who have lingered in their town—and see a common example of deprivation, poverty, and want. But somehow the men who have come from far away with stars in their eyes see something different. And they reveal to us what they see through their gifts.

We do the same, for good or ill. In the gifts that we give to Jesus the Christ, we reveal who we see him to be. Let that sink in. In the gifts we give to Jesus the Christ, we reveal who we see him to be. On this Epiphany day, who is Jesus to us?

The wise men have gone great distances and upended the normalcy of their lives to kneel at the feet of Jesus. With gold, frankincense, and myrrh they have acknowledged him as king, as priest, and as prophet. And then they give him their greatest gift. Knowing that Jesus' mission in the world depends upon them, they risk everything by defying King Herod. Rather than turning in Jesus to Herod, they leave town a different way. They change direction. As the sun does when one stares at it, the star in their eyes leaves an imprint they will carry for life, forming them into new people.

How far do we travel in our lives to kneel at the feet of Jesus? Do we set anything else aside, as the wise men set aside their entire lives, to make such time and room?

What do we bring him? Are our gifts perfunctory and frivolous, meaningless bobbles offered with little care or forethought? Or, do we set before Jesus the best of us: our passions, our love, our resources…all to acknowledge that he is king; that his body and blood save us; that he speaks the very voice of God?

And most importantly, when we look into the eyes of Christ, are our hearts moved to change direction? Do we stand up to those—even those with subtle or real power over us—and begin to walk in ways that support Jesus' mission in the world? Does the star in our eyes leave an imprint for life?

I mentioned earlier that those who were closest to the Holy Family in Bethlehem have trouble seeing Jesus for who he is. Sometimes that may be true of us as well. Jesus is a part of our culture and even our political in-fighting. We hear of Jesus and talk of Jesus so often—we are so close—that we may forget to look up and see that a heavenly sign rests above him. For us, too, as for the people in Bethlehem, the strange men from the East offer us a profound blessing in reminding us just who Jesus is. He is the king, around whom we should center our lives. He is the priest, through whose body and blood we are drawn close to God. He is the prophet, whose way of love can change our hearts and souls. This is who Jesus is revealed to be. And because he is all this to us, in the end we are the ones who have received the greatest gift.

Amen.

The Light That Dispels Fear

DECEMBER 2007   LUKE 2:1-20

TIn those days a decree went out from Emperor Augustus that all the world should be registered. This was the first registration and was taken while Quirinius was governor of Syria. All went to their own towns to be registered. Joseph also went from the town of Nazareth in Galilee to Judea, to the city of David called Bethlehem, because he was descended from the house and family of David. He went to be registered with Mary, to whom he was engaged and who was expecting a child. While they were there, the time came for her to deliver her child. And she gave birth to her firstborn son and wrapped him in bands of cloth, and laid him in a manger, because there was no place for them in the inn.

In that region there were shepherds living in the fields, keeping watch over their flock by night. Then an angel of the Lord stood before them, and the glory of the Lord shone around them, and they were terrified. But the angel said to them, 'Do not be afraid; for see—I am bringing you good news of great joy for all the people: to you is born this day in the city of David a Savior, who is the Messiah, the Lord. This will be a sign for you: you will find a child wrapped in bands of cloth and lying in a manger.'

And suddenly there was with the angel a multitude of the heavenly host, praising God and saying, 'Glory to God in the highest heaven, and on earth peace among those whom he favors!'

When the angels had left them and gone into heaven, the shepherds said to one another, 'Let us go now to Bethlehem and see this thing that has taken place, which the Lord has made known to us.' So they went with haste and found Mary and Joseph, and the child lying in the manger. When they saw this, they made known what had been told them about this child; and all who heard it were amazed at what the shepherds told them. But Mary treasured all these words and pondered them in her heart. The shepherds returned, glorifying and praising God for all they had heard and seen, as it had been told them.

The second chapter of Luke's Gospel may be the most beloved passage in all of Holy Scripture. We know it practically by heart. For many of us, whenever we hear it aloud—no matter who the speaker may be—it is Peanuts' Linus whose voice we hear, reciting on scratchy television film from the King James Version. We embrace this passage sentimentally, and it moves us like few others. But if we read it with care, we may be surprised to find that the emotion most present in the second chapter of Luke is not sentimentality but rather fear.

I am a father, and I remember the almost paralyzing anxiety associated with the birth of my first child, even though Jill and I benefited from a sterile, state-of-the-art obstetrics ward at a top-tier hospital. Now think of Joseph and Mary. Mary is uncomfortably pregnant and due to give birth, and yet she and Joseph must travel to a strange city, compelled there by the accident of Joseph's ancestry. Because he is of David's line, in order to be registered for Caesar's tax rolls he must go far from home to Bethlehem. (The tax code then was apparently as confusing as the tax code now!) Unlike the IRS, Caesar offers no extensions, and so despite the fact that Mary is due to give birth, Joseph must trek with her on the bumpy, uneven roads of Palestine. Even as they set out, the anxiety and fear surely begin to mount.

No relief comes with their arrival in Bethlehem. Caesar's decree has led to the inns being full, and the young couple is forced to accept the questionable shelter of a stable stall. No sooner have they laid down their packs in these inhospitable conditions than their worst case scenario comes to pass. Mary enters active labor, and fear must swell.

Like a compelling movie, the scene suddenly shifts to shepherds in the field outside of Bethlehem. We idealize the shepherds' vocation in stories and song, but in truth theirs is a life fraught with danger and fear. They live lonely for weeks on end in the wilderness, sometimes not even within sight of one another. They are hired hands who tend someone else's livelihood, fending off wolves and even lions with only so much as a staff. And this night is cold and lonely and devoid of light. The shepherds, too, though hardy and tough, are afraid.

And so we have Mary, who wraps her newborn child in bands of cloth, fearful for him in the cold; Joseph, who looks down at his young wife fearful of the complications that almost surely will come for her post-birth in such awful surroundings; and the shepherds, who tend the fields, fearful at every sound that wafts through the darkness. Not sentimentality, but fear pervades this passage.

Annie Dillard tells the story of a cold Christmas Eve during her childhood. Her family had come home late from dinner at a restaurant, and as she readied for bed there was a knock at the door. Her father opened the door, and standing at the threshold in the cold night air was Santa Claus himself. Rather than being filled with joy and excitement, Annie was struck with fear, and she turned and ran up the stairs. As she peeked down the banister, her father called to her to come down, but she was too afraid. She says:

> Like everyone in his right mind, I feared Santa Claus, thinking he was God.... [Santa Claus] knew when you'd been bad or good. He knew when you'd been bad or good! And I had been bad.

> My mother called and called, enthusiastic, pleading; I wouldn't come down.... I *couldn't* come down, but I could bend over the stairwell and see: Santa Claus stood in the doorway with night over his shoulder, letting in all the cold air of the sky; Santa Claus stood in the doorway monstrous and bright...repeating Merry Christmas, Merry Christmas. I never came down. I don't know who ate the cookies.[1]

Much later Annie realized that it was her widowed neighbor, Miss White, who had been dressed in the Santa suit that night. During Annie's childhood, Miss White was an incarnation of God for Annie, a woman who loved her and taught her encouraged her in the world. But that night, Annie knew only fear, and she ran.

Annie Dillard ends her story with a note to Miss White, or to God. She writes:

> I am sorry that I ran from you. I am still running, running from that knowledge, that eye, that love from which there is no refuge. For you meant only love and peace, and I felt fear.... So once in Israel love came to us incarnate, stood in the doorway between two worlds, and we were all afraid.[2]

Mary and Joseph are full of fear. The shepherds in the field are full of fear. The apprehension and anxiety almost leap from the page. But then a light pierces the darkness. It is so stunning and bright that all else melts away. And in that light the angel of the Lord appears. At first, the shepherds are even more fearful than they'd been before. They recoil like the young Annie Dillard running up the stairs. Luke says they are terrified. But then the angel speaks. He tells the shepherds about the birth of the child in the grime of the stable, a child who is also inexplicably the savior of the world. He explains that God himself has stepped into the doorway between the old world of fear and a new world of joy. The angel then beckons the shepherds forward to Bethlehem.

They can run away in their fear—as Annie Dillard claims we most often do when presented with the incarnate God, standing at the thresholds of our lives—or they can move toward that threshold and be received in joy.

The shepherds do not run. Fear is banished. They move into town to see the baby. They share the angel's words with Joseph and Mary, whose fear, too, is surely banished.

Mary, Joseph, the shepherds all, look at that baby and realize that God has opened a door, that in the newborn God the whole world truly stands at the threshold of a new age. And they are amazed.

At the stroke of midnight, though there will still be darkness, the night will have broken to morning. A new life will have entered into the world. As we approach the doorway of the church at the end of Holy Eucharist and look out into Christmas Day, we will truly stand in the threshold. On this day, love comes to us incarnate. His light pierces the darkness and shines for us and upon us. Can you feel it? We need not fear. We need not run away. Despite the cold air, if we will move through the threshold and into the new world, the newborn God will warm us heart and soul and carry us into new life. A child is born. Rejoice! Rejoice!

Amen.

ENDNOTES

1 Annie Dillard, *Teaching a Stone to Talk* (New York: HarperCollins, 1982), 138.

2 Ibid., 139.

Light in the Darkness

DECEMBER 2010   LUKE 2:1-20

In preparation for Christmas Eve services, the head usher and I huddled at the church's rather complex lighting panel to determine exactly what lighting combination would make the best mood for this service. Last weekend, as I sat enjoying seeing several parishioners perform in "My Son Pinocchio" at Mill Mountain Theatre, I turned on my smart phone's glowing viewscreen in order to see my playbill in the darkened theatre. Yesterday evening, when I took the dog out one last time before bed, I flipped the switch on our powerful backyard halogen lamp so I wouldn't stumble on any remaining patches of ice. The point is this: Never in my life—not for one moment—must I walk in darkness. Neither must you.

Consider that. Our access to light is so consistent and pervasive that we take it for granted above all else. For us, at midnight just as at noon, the light is never further away than the flip of a switch. Not so long ago, it was not so. As recently the 1600s, a full century after Henry VIII broke with Rome to establish the grand church tradition we call Anglicanism, no city on the planet was illuminated by night.[1] Forget those movie portrayals of medieval people walking down reliably torch-lit alleyways. Such images have no basis in fact. Long after the New World had been discovered and warfare was wrought with gunpowder, when the sun went down, the world was enshrouded in darkness. Absolute darkness. Hand-disappearing-in-front-of-your-face darkness. In cosmopolitan London just as in deepest Africa.

London finally created a system of nighttime illumination in the 1600s, but it wasn't until after the birth of this country in the late 1700s that gas lighting was invented, providing consistent and systematic light in the darkness. And it wasn't until around 1800 that the average Western European family could afford as a regular staple a stock of candles.

What I'm saying to you is this: Our experience of the world is incredibly new. We are able to fend off the night in ways that people as recently as two hundred years ago simply could not. Our eyes no longer widen in wonder when the candle's flame casts away shadows. We do not respond the way a young Robert Louis Stevenson did when his grandmother pulled him away from the window as he watched the lamplighter make his way down his London street lighting the gas lamps at murky dusk. "What are you doing?" asked the grandmother. And with bated breath the future poet and author replied, "I'm watching a man punch holes in the darkness."[2]

Once my wife Jill and I went on a camping excursion to a friend's hunting cabin. To call it a "cabin" is a stretch. It was a squat, square, concrete block enclosure with no windows. Once inside, when the lights were turned out, the darkness was absolute. Unexpectedly, I was claustrophobic. It was the rare experience that the darkness could reach out and smother me. That is what darkness was—regularly—for our ancestors: fearsome and inescapable.

Even more so during this time of year. The birth of Christ falls during the week of the winter solstice, when the day is shortest and the night encroaches most completely. In other words, in the middle of the night, on the longest night of the year, in the time of deepest darkness, Jesus is born.[3]

Forget soft and glowing drawings of doe-eyed lambs nuzzling Mary through a gentle labor. For one lying supine on the dirt about to give birth among caravan animals, the snorts and shuffles of large hoofed feet crowding around in the darkness would've added anxiety to an already fearful experience.

Of course, for the Holy Family as for so many others, the darkness was existential just as it was literal. The Jews of Palestine were an occupied people, kept under the boot of both a distant Roman Emperor and his local puppet Herod. Don't forget, Joseph was forced to travel in the middle of winter with a very pregnant wife to satisfy the caprice of Caesar Augustus. Joseph was not his own man.

And for the shepherds, the encroaching darkness was absolute. Shepherds and their sheep (which were practically blind even in daylight) regularly fell prey to wolves and even lions leaping from the darkness.

It is in this context that the baby enters the world. It is into this darkness that God takes on our humanity and arrives among us. It is here and now that the blackened sky parts over the shepherds in the field and the heavenly chorus erupts in song. That darkness, which every other night in human history had held sway, flees in their presence. The shepherds look on in utter wonder. The prowling creatures of the night retreat, the shepherds' fear melts, and they understand that with the birth of this child everything is made different. After all, what power can the night hold over the One who said in the beginning, "Let there be light"? When the angels of the Lord say, "Peace on earth among those whom God favors," the effect is that of Stevenson's lamplighter punching holes in the darkness.

In our outward lives, so long as the trusty smart phone is at hand, there is always at least a dim glow available. We no longer wonder at the presence of light. But existentially, we know what darkness is. As Marcus Borg says, "We easily get lost in the dark; we stumble around and cannot see our way. In the dark, we are often afraid. We do not know what might be going on: danger may lurk, spirits may roam, evil may be afoot."[4]

There are instances when the caprice of others—or of life itself—moves us where we do not want or need to go. There are times when heavy hooves push us about, knocking us to and fro and keeping us off balance. There are nights when we're barely able to keep the prowling creatures at bay.

But to us, too, Christ is born this night! No matter how thick the darkness, a light has entered the world that scatters all shadows. We've come back round to where we began: Truly, we need never walk in darkness! As Brennan Manning says with wonder like the shepherds, "The world is [now] charged with grace! While sin and war, disease and death are terribly real, God's loving presence and power in our midst are even more real."[5]

With the birth of this child, everything is made different. We are made different, as people visited by the angels with the promise of God's peace, as people commissioned like the shepherds to proclaim and share that peace.

What does it look like to live by the wonder of this light? When we travel into the meanest places and meet those who suffer want, do we dismiss them, or do we see in them the Holy Family and in their children the Christ child? When we see those who wander in their own darkness, do we pass them by, or do we step forward as with a shepherd's staff to fend of the prowling beasts and shepherd the blind to safety? When we feel the night falling upon us, do we cower, or do we look to the brightness of the Christ light and gravitate to its warmth?

When we leave this place, let us do so as if we're seeing the city illuminated by night for the first time. Let us do so with grins on our faces and light in our eyes, embracing those we meet, who may be stumbling around in murky dusk, and saying, "I have seen the child who punches holes in the darkness. He is born. Rejoice! Rejoice!"

Amen.

ENDNOTES

1 Marcus Borg and John Dominic Crossan, *The First Christmas: What the Gospels Really Teach About Jesus's Birth* (New York; HarperOne, 2007), 171-197.

2 This story was first told to me by the Very Rev. George Werner, former Dean of Trinity Cathedral in Pittsburgh.

3 Borg and Crossan, *The First Christmas*, 172.

4 Borg and Crossan, *The First Christmas*, 173.

5 Brennan Manning, *The Ragamuffin Gospel,* 3rd ed. (Colorado Springs, CO: Multnomah Books, 2005), 99.

Chasing Death from the Graveyard

APRIL 2010   JOHN 20:1-18

Early on the first day of the week, while it was still dark, Mary Magdalene came to the tomb and saw that the stone had been removed from the tomb. So she ran and went to Simon Peter and the other disciple, the one whom Jesus loved, and said to them, 'They have taken the Lord out of the tomb, and we do not know where they have laid him.' Then Peter and the other disciple set out and went towards the tomb. The two were running together, but the other disciple outran Peter and reached the tomb first. He bent down to look in and saw the linen wrappings lying there, but he did not go in. Then Simon Peter came, following him, and went into the tomb. He saw the linen wrappings lying there, and the cloth that had been on Jesus' head, not lying with the linen wrappings but rolled up in a place by itself. Then the other disciple, who reached the tomb first, also went in, and he saw and believed; for as yet they did not understand the scripture, that he must rise from the dead. Then the disciples returned to their homes.

But Mary stood weeping outside the tomb. As she wept, she bent over to look into the tomb; and she saw two angels in white, sitting where the body of Jesus had been lying, one at the head and the other at the feet. They said to her, 'Woman, why are you weeping?' She said to them, 'They have taken away my Lord, and I do not know where they have laid him.' When she had said this, she turned round and saw Jesus standing there, but she did not know that it was Jesus. Jesus said to her, 'Woman, why are you weeping? For whom are you looking?' Supposing him to be the gardener, she said to him, 'Sir, if you have carried him away, tell me where you have laid him, and I will take him away.' Jesus said to her, 'Mary!' She turned and said to him in Hebrew, 'Rabbouni!' (which means Teacher). Jesus said to her, 'Do not hold on to me, because I have not yet ascended to the Father. But go to my brothers and say to them, "I am ascending to my Father and your Father, to my God and your God." ' Mary Magdalene went and announced to the disciples, 'I have seen the Lord'; and she told them that he had said these things to her.

I'm going to go way out on a limb and begin an Easter sermon with a Halloween story. That's not what you'd expect, is it? But then again, this day is all about the unexpected.

In some cities, the town grows up around a courthouse square, university quad, or a river. In my hometown of Paragould, Arkansas, the town surrounds and extends from a massive graveyard, Linwood Cemetery. When I was growing up this didn't occur to me as odd, but now when I go home I'm momentarily startled to drive into the heart of town and see this huge bone garden that covers so much real estate.

For several years when I was in elementary school, my brother Robert, his best friend, and I hosted a huge Halloween party. Some woods separated our house from the friend's, and we'd spend days raking trails through the woods in preparation for all sorts of scary party games on Halloween night. But one year it occurred to us that in no way could the forest ever be as scary on All Hallows Eve as Linwood Cemetery. We begged our moms to take us all into the graveyard to tell ghost stories on Halloween night after dark.

That year I dressed as a Crusader knight. (Even then I was a church nerd.) I had a purple tunic, wool leggings of my Mom's that I thought resembled chainmail—this was 1980, after all—and a wooden sword I'd spray painted silver.

On Halloween night, my mother and a couple of other moms led a menagerie of costumed kids down the road and into the cemetery. There were probably thirty of us. The moms wanted to stop at the gate, but we insisted on walking deep into the graveyard, stopping only when we reached the mammoth mausoleum in its center. We stopped, sat down, and began telling ghost stories.

Now, unbeknownst to us some kid's high school-aged older brother had heard about our plans. And for days he'd apparently been making plans of his own. He set up a cassette player behind the mausoleum and began playing a tape of shrieks and screams. We froze. Then he jumped out from the bushes wearing green coveralls, a Jason Voorhees hockey mask from "Friday the 13th" (which had just come out in theaters a few months before), and brandishing a chainsaw (without the chain). I remember my mother screaming, which is what the high school hooligan hoped for and expected. I'm pretty sure he didn't expect what happened next.

Fortified with punch and Halloween cookies, the kid next to me jumped to his feet and yelled, "Get him!" I realized I was carrying a sword, and I added, "Charge!" With that, thirty elementary school kids ran headlong for Jason in the hockey mask, waving our pitchforks, witches' brooms, and cap guns as we went. For just a second Jason stood dumbstruck in disbelief—as though someone had risen from the grave—dropping the chainsaw to his side. Then he took off, running away from us as fast as he could through the cemetery. We never did find out whose big brother he was. Apparently, kids in high school don't brag about it when a gang of third-graders terrifies them on Halloween. Plus, we went home with very nice cassette recorder.

We felt as if we'd chased death itself from the graveyard. That night in the darkness, things went down in the graveyard in the most unexpected ways.

Usually, we know what to expect when we visit the cemetery. We go there to visit those who've gone, to remember what is past and pine for what will never be. Loss smoothed by time pierces again as we walk among the tombs.

Frederick Niedner adds that "unfinished business [also] lingers in every graveyard—broken promises, betrayals, countless secrets left to perish with the departed. Sometimes visitors speak to the dead. They apologize, even plead for absolution, but none comes. Silence stands guard. The stone will never be rolled away."[1]

Whether the graveyard stands literally in the center of town or figuratively in the center of our souls, it symbolizes the wrongs we cannot right, broken vows we cannot mend, the hopes crushed under the weight of the world and buried under heavy stone.

Such weight is carried by the women as they approach Jesus' tomb in the darkness before dawn this morning. Two days ago they saw the hope of their hearts dragged from prayer in the Garden of Gethsemane. Rather than rallying to his aid, the women saw the men closest to Jesus run away in fear. The women watched, helpless and in horror, as Jesus was paraded through the streets and crucified on a barren hill outside of town.

Surely they pause at the cemetery gate early on Easter morning, frightened of the graveyard in the dark. But on they walk, deep among the tombs, until they reach the mausoleum of their friend and teacher. And then, that morning in the darkness, things go down in the graveyard in the most unexpected ways.

This time, finally, God will not allow the stone to hold the dead. When grief for an only son touches the heart of God, it is like phosphorous coming into contact with water. The reaction is powerful and swift. The universe is shaken. God sends his angels costumed in dazzling clothes to charge against death, chasing death from the graveyard, and shattering the darkness with light. The stone is rolled away, and the grave is empty. The Son of God lives.

He was dead, and with him died all of our wrongs, the promises we have broken and those that have broken us, the disappointments that drown our hopes. Jesus has taken these things down to the grave. But though he leaves them buried there, he himself returns to us. He's come back without them.

I know it's confusing. The women were confused. And when they returned to the disciples, the disciples were confused, too. Luke uses the word "amazement" to describe their reaction. They've spent the past few days grieving the death of hope, and it will take time to understand how to live with resurrected hope that cannot die.

We've had a lot longer to get used to our grief than they had. In some cases we've had years to settle into the sorrow of our disappointments, and we may be oddly comfortable among the tombs. But friends, Jesus is alive, and we can live anew with him and in him. We can give to him all those things that weigh on us in the graveyard of our hearts: all the things we're ashamed of, the things we wish we'd done differently, the things about us even now that threaten to pull us underground. Jesus will put even those into the tomb and return us to life.

If we will embrace Easter—beginning today, but giving ourselves dedicated time beyond today to really grasp what it means—then even visits to actual cemeteries will become very different affairs. We'll visit the graves of those who've gone clothed in our new lives. We'll share with them now in hope and love, rather than wistfulness and regret, what God is doing within us, transforming us into new creatures. And then, perhaps, we'll even be able to resurrect our broken relationships with the living, sharing with them how what was dead in us is gone and what remains lives with hope anew.

Yes, indeed, beginning today in the graveyard, things are going down in the most unexpected ways!

Amen.

ENDNOTES

1 Frederick Niedner, "Living by the Word: Rejoice, Believers," *The Christian Century* (March 11, 2008): 21.

Sleepers, Wake!

APRIL 2011

JOHN 20:1-18

In an old, long ago-polished wooden box at home, I keep a stack of letters written in the 1950s, when an Air Mail stamp cost 3 cents. The letters are brittle and yellowed, and they are penned in a script from a bygone era, when penmanship was itself an art. Written in Enid, Oklahoma, and posted to Houston, Texas, the first letter in the stack, dated December 31, 1950, begins joyously, with stories of the holidays and hopes for the new decade. Soon, though, the letters' foreshadowing darkens. One woman writing to another tells of the increasing health concerns of her husband. By early 1956, that husband has himself traveled from Enid to Houston to be under the care of a hotshot young heart surgeon named Michael DeBakey. Before the patient can be stabilized for experimental heart surgery, he dies. The final letter in the stack, dated June 5, 1956, is written not from Enid but from McGehee, Arkansas, where the forty-six year old widow and her young son have moved home to be with her family. This letter, so starkly different from the holiday epistle which began the series six years earlier, says this:

> [I] hardly know where to begin. Everything is such a mess. Furniture is badly worn, walls dirty, and etc. Every time I begin to concentrate on a specific job three or four people drop in and I get delayed...Everything in the apartment reminds me of [him]. I don't like to stop moving or be by myself. Life seems so empty that I nearly forget to count my blessings.

Light has gone from the young woman's life. It is as if her eyes have closed, and she has fallen asleep.

In the first third of the 20th Century, the most fertile missionary ground on earth—the shining light of missionary zeal—was China. Seven thousand Christian missionaries poured into the country and established hundreds of hospitals and thousands of schools, converting the Chinese to the Christian faith along the way. When the Communists under Chairman Mao finally chased Chiang Kai-Shek off the mainland in 1949, events were set in motion that resulted in all Christian missionaries leaving virtually overnight. As the best-hearted fled, they worried and prayed for the some four million Chinese Christians they were leaving behind, and with good cause. Chairman Mao's wife made it her personal mission to stamp out Christianity in China. Chinese Christians found themselves imprisoned, "re-educated" in special camps, and in some gruesome instances even crucified with nails driven through their palms. Light had gone from the mission field, and it was as if Christian China had fallen asleep.[1]

On June 28, 2008, twelve-year-old Hunter Grove let go of the ski rope on Smith Mountain Lake in southwestern Virginia and careened head-first into a dock. His father Carl, who was driving the boat, watched the scene over his shoulder in horror. By the time he made it to Hunter, the boy was unconscious and bleeding from his ears. Hunter was airlifted to Charlottesville, and the doctors' prognosis was grim. Quite literally, the light had gone from Hunter's life. He had fallen asleep and could not wake up.

Hearing any of these stories, Mary Magdalene would say, "Yes! I know what that is. I know what it is for the light to go out. I know what it is to fall asleep and lose all hope."

Like the Christian missionaries in China, Mary's fortunes changed from zeal to terror overnight. Like Hunter Grove's father, Mary witnessed in horror the devastation of the one she loved the very most, helpless to step in and stop his pain. Like the young widow in Arkansas, Mary wandered about in the aftermath, not sure in her emptiness what to do or where to find meaning.

The Sabbath over, Mary goes to Jesus' tomb dazed and confused. She goes there because even after the crucifixion Jesus' body suffered the added indignity of burial without proper anointing. She has come to do the only thing she can think to do: apply aromatic spices to her beloved's body in a final, furtive, desperate act of love. But when Mary arrives at the tomb, Jesus is not there. In her virtual sleepwalking, she becomes frantic to find him, and she almost collides headlong with a man she assumes to be the gardener. "Please, give him back!" she pleads.

And then the man standing before Mary speaks. There is an Easter hymn sung to an Irish tune that says, "The most precious Word of Life / cleared his throat and ended silence." It is Jesus the Christ standing before her, alive.

In every conceivable way, Mary's eyes are opened. The darkness flees. She wakes up from the emptiness. And in that moment she is, just as surely as Jesus is, resurrected. In all the Gospel post-Easter resurrection stories, it is the same. Those asleep and walking in darkness have their eyes opened by the presence of the risen Jesus, and they experience their own resurrection.

Hunter Grove woke up weeks after the accident on Smith Mountain Lake. It was weeks later still that he began to speak and months before he could walk. But all these things he did. Seven months after his accident, with a long road of recovery still ahead of him, Hunter himself said, "When I was dead and my eyes were dead, I couldn't hear what you were saying, but I remember you holding my hand."

Somehow through that darkness, Easter came!

Fifty years after the Christian missionaries were expelled from China, some were finally allowed to return under strict limitations. They landed in China in virtual hopelessness. But they found that the four million Christians they had to abandon half a century before had burgeoned to eighty million, a thriving church who gathered not in comfort but under assault and who knew of what they spoke when they proclaimed each and every week, "Jesus lives!"

Somehow in that closed-off land, Easter came!

I have one other letter in that wooden box at home. It is written in 1962 from my grandmother to my father, who was by then a sophomore in college. The earlier letters are so hard for me to read, because my grandmother was the most faithful person I ever knew. Fifty-five years removed, her emptiness and hopelessness after my grandfather's death in 1956 still bring me to tears. And yet, the 1962 letter is the testimony of a Christian wide-awake, one who sees the world with open eyes through the light of the living Christ. This letter, motherly advice to a barely-grown son, ends with these words:

> Your happiness will come from within and not from material things. Unless you live close to God life will not be worth living, but with Him anything can be accomplished. You can take any hardship life deals you as long as He is at your side...My life has been beautiful and I have loved every minute of it.

Somewhere in the Good Friday between 1956 and 1962, Easter came.

Sleepers, wake! The world is ablaze with light. Jesus lives this day. He is resurrected, and his resurrection will meet us in whatever sorrow, whatever pain, whatever darkened world in which we find ourselves. The great Church Father Gregory of Nazianzus proclaims for all of us:

> Yesterday I was crucified with Christ; today I am glorified in him. Yesterday I was dead with Christ; today I am sharing in his resurrection. Yesterday I was buried with him; today I am waking with him from the sleep of death.[2]

The Lord is risen, indeed!

Amen.

ENDNOTES

1 Philip Yancey, *What Good is God?: In Search of a Faith that Matters* (Brentwood, TN: FaithWords, 2010), 41-52.

2 *Common Prayer: Services and Prayers for the Church of England* (London: Church House Publishing, 2005), 76.

Spirit

I Am Coming!

MAY 2007   JOHN 14:18, 27-28

I will not leave you orphaned; I am coming to you. Peace I leave with you; my peace I give to you. I do not give to you as the world gives. Do not let your hearts be troubled, and do not let them be afraid. You heard me say to you, "I am going away, and I am coming to you."

In October 1987 news crackled along the airwaves of an event that for 58 hours mesmerized the nation. In Midland, Texas, an eighteen-month-old little girl had been playing outside of her aunt's house when her mother stepped into the house to answer the telephone. When the mother returned outdoors, her daughter had disappeared. As the mother looked around the yard for the little girl, she noticed an opening in the ground no wider than a dessert plate. At first, she passed by this tiny opening without giving it a second thought, but as it became clear that her daughter was gone and could not have toddled far, a sense of horror washed over the woman. The eight-inch opening was an uncapped well. The little girl had fallen deep into the ground, so far that all around her was darkness.

The ordeal of Baby Jessica, as the little girl came to be known, was simply one of thousands in which children were endangered that year. Most barely made the local paper. What was it about this particular event that electrified so many people? What made so many of us—myself included—crowd around television sets for two and a half days until we were bleary-eyed? I believe that at root we were captivated by fear, not just the fear for our own children but a fear that lurks deep in each of our individual hearts, a fear that Baby Jessica, all of eighteen-months-old, faced during those dark days: the fear of being utterly, completely alone.

This may lie at the root of all our fears. Those who say they fear public speaking usually mean that they fear being isolated and alone in front of a crowd of people. Put them in an ensemble, and their fear subsides. Those who say they fear the dark are often quite comfortable in darkness so long as they are in the arms of another. And those who fear death often shy away not from the pain of dying (though that is surely daunting, too) but from the realization that in leaving this earth we must do it alone, stripped of the companionship of those people who have walked through all else in life with us. In the depths of our being, we fear being starkly, desperately alone.

This is what the disciples fear in John's Gospel today. It is after supper, and Jesus has been talking to the disciples for some time. As he has spoken, the disciples have slowly come to the realization that what Jesus is doing is saying goodbye. The air becomes thick with emotion; reactions and responses from the disciples to Jesus become awkward. We've all experienced those moments when someone you love must go, perhaps for a long time or forever, and the final few minutes together become surreal. You want to say so much that hasn't been said. You want to hold your loved one frozen in time so as not to let her go. For the disciples, all of these emotions and experiences are compounded because Jesus is their love, their leader, their inspiration, and the glue that holds them together.

The disciples begin to imagine their lives shaped by Jesus' absence, and the image is terrifying to them. As Gail O'Day puts it, "they fear that they will be left like children without parents, with no one to care for them, with no one to love and no one to love them."[1] Jesus is going, they realize, and they fear being alone.

As the hours wore on with Baby Jessica in the ground, I remember the drillers working with excruciating slowness to bore a rescue shaft alongside the well. Finally, the new tunnel was deep enough that rescue workers could be lowered within earshot of the little girl. When one came back to the surface, caked in sweat and grime, a reporter asked what the rescuer had said to Jessica.

"I'm coming!" he replied, "I told her, 'Hold on! I'm coming!'"

It was still hours before the little girl was recovered from the darkness. Her ordeal was still long from over. But in that moment, for her and for all of us watching, something crucial in the dynamic had changed. The child was no longer alone. She was held in the promise that someone was coming for her, that she was not forgotten nor consigned to the darkness. Her heart need not be troubled, and she need not be afraid.

In the upper room, as the disciples succumb to their fear of being alone, Jesus offers these and other words. He says to them, "I will not leave you orphaned."

"I am going away," Jesus says, "But I am coming to you! Do not let your hearts be troubled. Do not be afraid. I am coming!"

Jesus promises that though he must leave, his Spirit will return to live with those who love him, to be a loving presence in all darkness, to be a comfort in all fear, to be a strength in all adversity.

We, like the apostles, are a fearful people, skittish and terrified of being alone. We lose loved ones. Our families breakdown. We face medical challenges. We suffer professional disappointments. We barely hold it all together in the face of our trepidation about being alone.

But then the words of the Gospel ring out today. Like the rescuer in Midland, Texas, "I'm coming!" cries God to each of us. "I'm coming!" cries Jesus who, hanging on the cross, understands our fear of being alone. "I'm coming!" cries the Spirit whom God sends, who bursts through those very windows and those very doors and into the bread and wine on this table. And into our hearts.

For many, this message will resonate. You will have experienced the indwelling of the Spirit of Christ in the Eucharist and in your hearts. Others I can imagine are thinking, "That's all fine and good, but at times when the walls seem to be falling down around me and I am all alone, I could do with something more tangible than my own warmed heart!"

What I would offer in response is that I haven't used the story of Baby Jessica in the well as a metaphor only. Looking back on those 58 hours, twenty years ago in Midland, Texas, the Spirit of God arrived through the tireless love and labor of real human beings: drillers, firemen, EMTs, and countless praying people. The Spirit lived in the form of the community, symbolized in the person of that grubby EMT who spoke for them all and proclaimed to a terrified child, "Hold on! I am coming!"

In the fourteenth chapter of John's Gospel, much of what Jesus claims about the Spirit is that it will live through the community of those who love Jesus, in other words, the church. Thinking back to all those human fears that I mentioned at the beginning, those that have at their root the fear of being alone, the church is the ensemble among whom we need never fear standing alone. The church offers the arms that will hold us safe in the darkness. The church is the Body of Christ who will be with us on this side of dying and pray for us as we enter into the arms of Christ on death's other side.

For fifty-eight solid hours, the Spirit dwelt with Baby Jessica in her heart and in the people who stood with her, and she was not alone. That is the promise we share. Let not our hearts be troubled, and let us not be afraid. Jesus Christ will not leave us orphaned. *We* will not leave *one another* standing alone. For we know that the Spirit is coming to us, and indeed the Spirit is already here.

Amen.

ENDNOTES

1 Gail O'Day, "John," vol. IX of *The New Interpreter's Bible* (Nashville, TN:Abingdon Press, 1995), 753.

Rosencrantz and Guildenstern are Dead

MAY 2009   ACTS 2:1-21

When the day of Pentecost had come, they were all together in one place. And suddenly from heaven there came a sound like the rush of a violent wind, and it filled the entire house where they were sitting. Divided tongues, as of fire, appeared among them, and a tongue rested on each of them. All of them were filled with the Holy Spirit and began to speak in other languages, as the Spirit gave them ability...

I've always liked Rosencrantz and Guildenstern. You remember them, right? They're characters in Shakespeare's *Hamlet*. Rosencrantz and Guildenstern are Prince Hamlet's childhood friends, and in the shady, psychological drama that crescendos between Hamlet and his Uncle Claudius, Rosencrantz and Guildenstern attempt to jockey their way to favor and advance. But the two never really understand what's going on around them. They are darkly comical in that way. They have great self-confidence, and they perceive themselves to be working the system to their own advantage, passing secrets to Claudius while using velvet language to curry Hamlet's good graces. But their perception is all wrong. In truth, they are peripheral characters. The action they think they are influencing really swirls around them, buffeting them in ways they don't even recognize. They are sideshows in the story at best, not really part of it in any meaningful way. In the end, Rosencrantz and Guildenstern find themselves on a ship as messengers ignorantly carrying a letter that instructs the King of England to kill them. After all their ludicrous machinations, they finally succeed in this, and an ambassador later reports back to Denmark the famous line, "Rosencrantz and Guildenstern are dead." And no one cares. The play's action simply continues as before.

As is so often the case, themes and characters in Shakespeare's plays resonate with Scripture. The bumbling, self-important, peripheral Rosencrantz and Guildenstern are not unlike Jesus' twelve disciples. Though we tend to idealize the twelve, even a cursory reading of the Gospels exposes them as, well, bumbling, self-important, and peripheral. They get in the way and impede Jesus' ministry more often than they provide real support. When Jesus is exhausted, they badger him like backseat children pestering a wearied parent on a long drive. When Jesus patiently teaches them, they respond by arguing over who will be his top lieutenant. When Jesus, with a hopeful twinkle in his eyes, nudges them from the nest with a task for ministry, they return complaining that other good people are out there doing God's work and getting in their way. And finally, when Jesus is abducted on Maundy Thursday, the twelve flee like King Arthur's men in *Monty Python and the Holy Grail*. ("Run away!") At times the Gospel writers may intend for the twelve to provide some darkly comic relief. Like Costello to Abbott, they just can't grasp what Jesus is all about. It's as if Jesus speaks a language they cannot comprehend. Despite the fact that they hear him so often, in many ways they are never really part of his story.

Until today. This is the pivotal day in the life of the twelve, in the life of the Christian faith, in the life of the Church. This is the day that peripheral characters become main characters. This is the day when the followers of Jesus learn to speak the language of his story.

The change is major, not minor. It's thunderous, not quiet. It's like the din of a bell banner unexpectedly processed into church, or the surprise of a Gospel text read simultaneously in a dozen different languages. *Every* expectation is upended. *Everything* changes. By just how much, we'll see.

Today the disciples gather in faith—not just the twelve, but 120 followers of Jesus that Luke has mentioned earlier in his Gospel. They congregate for the festival of Pentecost, fifty days after the Passover. And while they are together, the Spirit of God enters the house. The Spirit appears among them, flowing between and through them, changing the atmosphere, like the crackle of lightening on an unstable night. What had been merely a gathering place becomes *ekklesia*— church—and those who had been extras become main characters in the drama. This change is most potently manifest when the language of God's story—the language of the Spirit—becomes, quite literally, their language.

Disciples from all over the known world are there, and though at first they all seem to be babbling incoherently, slowly ears are opened and each person present can understand their words as if those words are being spoken directly to each heart. The language of the Spirit becomes a shared language, and it becomes on that day the language by which they all define their very lives.

Luke drives this home at the end of today's reading, when Peter stands up and speaks above the crowd. This is the same Peter who jockeyed for Jesus' ear by day and cowered in the shadows by night. The language by which Peter's life had been defined was all about how being a follower of Jesus might benefit Peter. But now he stands and gives voice not to the desires of his own heart but to the message of salvation. He calls upon all those present to listen and heed the Gospel. And the language Peter begins to speak on this day will be his language every day for the remainder of his life.

As with Rosencrantz and Guildenstern, as with the twelve disciples, so with us. We live, for the most part, as extras in God's story. We prioritize our lives according to languages other than God's: the language of economic prosperity and consumption, the language of epicurean desire and instant gratification, the twenty-first century American language of self-defining and self-centered individualism that says my wants and comforts in life come first. We even co-opt God into the stories we weave with our language, giving him a supporting role and pretending that he conveniently wants for us all the same things we want for ourselves.

As with the disciples, the language of God's story strikes us as so odd we first consider it quizzically and may then disregard it altogether. We come to church occasionally, but we're confused as to why. We try to pray every once in a while, but unless we're praying for things we want—co-opting God into our stories again—we're not sure the reason. We want our kids to be raised in faith (it seems vaguely important to us that they be), but the life of faith tends far down on our list of priorities.

Rosencrantz and Guildenstern attempted simply to graft Hamlet's drama into their own. The disciples attempted to interpret the Gospel according to the language by which they already lived their lives. We seek to compartmentalize our faith as one (usually minor) piece of us, alongside our jobs, our families, our extracurricular activities, our spare time.

But the Spirit doesn't work that way. The disciples learned on Pentecost that God will not be made a character in some other story. God's language is primary. It interprets all else, and not the other way around. The language of the Spirit binds people—the disciples in that house and us in this one—as more than acquaintances, more than friends…as a holy family. The language of the Spirit changes us from sidelines extras into main characters in God's drama. It's a language that redefines the way we do our jobs, the way we pray, the way we prioritize the things in our lives. It's a language that says, first, "*I am God's.* His Spirit enters me, soothes me, shakes me. I am God's, first and foremost, and all the things in my life are an open response to his Gospel." When we speak this language to each other and to a hungry world, ears will open! When we speak with Peter's courage, lives will be saved.

Beginning on Pentecost, there is no part of the disciples' lives left untouched by God. His spirit permeates them like the very air they breathe. Never again will they run away. Never again will they quit in confusion. Today, God's Spirit enters this place. This is the birthday of the Church. It can be your birthday in faith; it can be mine. This very day can be the day that you become a main character in God's story, in every part of your life.

Rosencrantz and Guildenstern are dead; in us the Spirit of God may come to life.

Amen

Images of the Spirit

JUNE 2011   ACTS 2:1-21 & ROMANS 8:14-17

When the day of Pentecost had come, they were all together in one place. And suddenly from heaven there came a sound like the rush of a violent wind, and it filled the entire house where they were sitting. Divided tongues, as of fire, appeared among them, and a tongue rested on each of them. All of them were filled with the Holy Spirit and began to speak in other languages, as the Spirit gave them ability...

For all who are led by the Spirit of God are children of God. For you did not receive a spirit of slavery to fall back into fear, but you have received a spirit of adoption. When we cry, 'Abba! Father!' it is that very Spirit bearing witness with our spirit that we are children of God, and if children, then heirs, heirs of God and joint heirs with Christ—if, in fact, we suffer with him so that we may also be glorified with him.

It all started innocently enough. A casual phone call was placed to the principal of Ridgecrest High School by a local minister who had heard that Elvis Presley's first cousin would be coming through Paragould. He was a motivational speaker for youth it seems, and he could stop by the high school and pepper his student talk with anecdotes about Elvis, who he'd apparently actually even met once at a family reunion of some sort. Forgetting for a moment that kids in 1988 were tuned to the music of Prince, Tears for Fears, and Van Halen rather than Elvis, the principal thought this sounded like a great idea, and Elvis' cousin was invited to the school.

With four hundred-fifty kids squeezed into the high school auditorium, Elvis' cousin told jokes, made faces, and generally encouraged us to stay in school. Then, at the end, he off-handedly remarked that he would be speaking again that night at the local church whose minister had initially tipped off our principal. We could come hear him then, too, if we'd like, and there'd be free pizza.

We must have been having meatloaf at my house that night, because my brother and his best friend decided they'd attend. Their first steps though the doors of this unfamiliar church revealed that this was different from that to which they were accustomed. What they saw was a group of youth parading around the fellowship hall in a sort of conga line and a frenetic youth director cavorting around them crying, "Feel that Holy Spirit! Everyone join the Loooooove Train!" The kids in the conga line had Cheshire cat grins on their faces, rapt by both the dance and the encouragement of their leader. My brother and his friend were for a moment frozen like deer in headlights, but then the smell of pepperoni wafted across their noses and they thought, "When in Rome..." and joined the love train.

After supper but before my brother could make a break for his 1984 Chevy Citation hatchback, all the kids were ushered into the church's sanctuary. On the stage Elvis' cousin appeared, but he was no longer the face-making teller of jokes. Instead, he was overcome with the Holy Ghost, and in a spirit-filled frenzy he preached, pranced, threw his hands skyward, and had side conversations with God for the better part of an hour. Eventually, my brother and his friend crept to the edge of their pew and began to slink toward the back of the church to make their escape. Cousin Elvis caught sight of them, pointed a finger and bellowed, "You kids better sit down and pay attention, because this is what heaven is going to be like!"

Later when my brother told me all about his experience, I was glad I'd stayed home and had the meatloaf.

My brother's experience isn't too far off the mark, I suspect, from what comes to many of our minds when we consider the Holy Spirit. With God we are comfortable. With Jesus we can kind of relate. But the Holy Spirit? Acts adds that at the first Christian Pentecost the Spirit appeared as the "rush of a violent wind" and "tongues of fire" that rested on the gathered crowd. The images of the Spirit with which we most often come into contact are discomfiting at least and downright disturbing at most.

It should be said that our discomfort does not mean that these images of the Spirit are off-base or untrue. Though I might offer a critique of his work with youth, I would not claim that Elvis' cousin lacked a true connection to the Holy Spirit. The Spirit of God will not be constrained by our comfort zones. The Spirit is at times wild and mystifying, and the trouble of our coming to grips with that Spirit is our trouble rather than God's.

The real problem for those of us for whom these manifestations of the Spirit feel so foreign is that we are left wondering, "Does the Holy Spirit have anything to do with me? Am I defective in some way, because I am more comfortable with liturgy rather than the "love train," with quiet prayer instead of frenzied speaking in tongues?"

You are not defective, and neither am I. And despite the reading from Acts that we hear each Pentecost Sunday—or perhaps *in addition to it*—there are other images of the Spirit that may resonate for us. I'd like to share a few with you.

The first is shared by John Wesley, founder of the Methodists, who was himself a good Anglican priest until the day he died. At a Moravian meeting on Aldersgate Street in London in1738, Wesley found that the Holy Spirit touched even him. This is what he recorded of the event:

> In the evening, I went *very unwilling* to a society in Aldersgate Street were one was reading Luther's "Preface" to the Epistle to the Romans. About a quarter before nine, while he was describing the change which God works in the heart through faith in Christ, *I felt my heart strangely warmed.* I felt that I did trust in Christ, Christ alone for salvation, and an assurance was given me, that he had taken away my sins, even mine, and saved me from the law of sin and death.[1]

Notice what happened here. On this night Wesley felt both tug and resistance simultaneously. He did not want to go and be among this group of Moravians, and yet God's Spirit beckoned him subtly and would not leave him alone. Once there, Wesley experienced a comforting presence of which no one was aware but himself. There was no dramatic display, only the warming of his heart.

The invitation to be moved spiritually in a new way; the comfort of God's presence— that is the Holy Spirit.

The second image is in the Book of Exodus, where Moses leads the people Israel out of bondage in Egypt, through the Red Sea, and toward the Promised Land. But there's one catch: before Canaan can be reached, the Israelites must traverse the wilderness. By day, the terrain is rocky and treacherous. A wrong turn and the people could be injured or lost. By night, the landscape is inky black, and all manner of demons seem to lash out from the darkness. When the Israelites don't know how to move forward, God's Spirit comes to them in their need, offering a pillar of cloud by day and a pillar of fire by night, "to lead them on their way," Exodus says, "and give them light." The Apostle Paul adds to this in Romans that "all who are led by the Spirit of God are children of God."

Guidance through the treacherous terrain of life—the intuition that gives us compass during the day, and the hope that grants us light in all darkness—that is the Holy Spirit.

A final image: A man who had been a fairly active member of his parish has all but stopped coming to church. On a brisk winter evening his old priest comes to visit, and the man invites the priest in. They sit in front of the glowing fire.

"It's not that I have anything against the church, Father," the man says, "I've just decided to focus on me in my life. I'm not unreligious, but I can experience God when I'm by myself working or fishing or anything else just as much as when I'm with people from the church."

The old priest sits silently in front of the fire, and both of them slowly become mesmerized by the glowing embers. Within the fire, it is almost impossible to distinguish one log from another. Surely, each log is a separate piece of wood, but the fire that passes through and between them becomes one glow that binds them together.

Without saying a word, the old priest takes the fireplace tongs and lifts a small piece of wood off of the fire. He sets it on the hearth apart from the rest of the glowing logs. For a while this small, now separated piece of wood dances and flickers within with the same glow as the greater fire. Slowly, though, the solitary ember dims and then loses its color and becomes cold.

"Only when the embers live together can the fire live in the wood," the priest finally says and then looks intently at his friend, "And remember, the fire burns not only for its own sake, but for those outside who seek relief from the cold."

With that the priest reaches forward and with his bare hands picks up the cold, charred small piece of wood off of the hearth. He tosses it back into the fire, and immediately it glows with light and heat again. He stands up and shakes hands with his host, offering him a broad smile and going on his way.[2]

The life-giving fire and energy of the gathered Church, which are experienced by its members both for their own sake and as a witness to a world grown cold and hard with cynicism and despair—that is the Holy Spirit.

Comfort, guidance, energy, and our life together. These are the Holy Spirit. We rarely name them as such, but it is time we began. The Spirit comes to us everyday in moments of reflection, doubt, decision, and fellowship. It comes again today, for today is Pentecost.

Amen.

ENDNOTES

1 John Wesley, *Journal* for 24 May 1738, in *Journals and Diaries I (1735-1738)*, vol. 18 of the *Bicentennial Edition of the Works of John Wesley*, edited by W. Reginald Ward and Richard P. Heitzenrater (Nashville, TN:Abingdon Press, 1988), 249-250.

2 I first heard this story during my childhood from the Rev. Jim Keith at the First United Methodist Church of Paragould, Arkansas. I have been told by a parishioner that the Rev. Leighton Ford, one-time colleague of Billy Graham, employed a similar anecdote in a sermon entitled "One Log Doesn't Burn Alone." I have been unable to locate the Rev. Ford's sermon, but I'm pleased to offer conditional attribution to him.

Discipleship

Faithful Friends

JUNE 2010   2 KINGS 2:1-2, 6-14

Now when the LORD was about to take Elijah up to heaven by a whirlwind, Elijah and Elisha were on their way from Gilgal. Elijah said to Elisha, 'Stay here; for the LORD has sent me as far as Bethel.' But Elisha said, 'As the LORD lives, and as you yourself live, I will not leave you.' So they went down to Bethel.

Then Elijah said to him, 'Stay here; for the LORD has sent me to the Jordan.' But he said, 'As the LORD lives, and as you yourself live, I will not leave you.' So the two of them went on. Fifty men of the company of prophets also went, and stood at some distance from them, as they both were standing by the Jordan. Then Elijah took his mantle and rolled it up, and struck the water; the water was parted to the one side and to the other, until the two of them crossed on dry ground.

When they had crossed, Elijah said to Elisha, 'Tell me what I may do for you, before I am taken from you.' Elisha said, 'Please let me inherit a double share of your spirit.' He responded, 'You have asked a hard thing; yet, if you see me as I am being taken from you, it will be granted you; if not, it will not.' As they continued walking and talking, a chariot of fire and horses of fire separated the two of them, and Elijah ascended in a whirlwind into heaven. Elisha kept watching and crying out, 'Father, father! The chariots of Israel and its horsemen!' But when he could no longer see him, he grasped his own clothes and tore them in two pieces.

He picked up the mantle of Elijah that had fallen from him, and went back and stood on the bank of the Jordan. He took the mantle of Elijah that had fallen from him, and struck the water, saying, 'Where is the LORD, the God of Elijah?' When he had struck the water, the water was parted to the one side and to the other, and Elisha went over.

The darkness of outer space crowds around the star pilot as he careens down the trench. Right behind him are three ships—Tie Fighters, to be exact—that wish him dead. With each laser blast fired in his direction, they get a bit closer to their mark. All those friends who had been alongside him are gone. He is naked in the dark, so to speak. Just when hope is all but lost, the camera pans up to reveal another ship, a familiar one, haloed in the corona of a nearby sun. Not all friends have abandoned him after all! One has remained. The faithful friend scatters the enemy, and our hero is able to complete his mission.

The hero, of course, is Luke Skywalker. The darkness of space surrounds his X-Wing Fighter and the Death Star, and the friend who at the last minute faithfully stands—or flies—beside him in the Millennium Falcon is Han Solo. Whether you saw Star Wars in the theater in 1977 as I did or on digitally remastered DVD as my children have, that final scene, when Han Solo remains faithful to his friend in the nick of time, makes the heart swell and lifts the spirit.

There is mythic truth in the scene on two levels: First, we fear nothing so much, in the end, as being alone. Second, we so yearn for the faithful friend and partner who will not leave us naked in the darkness that no matter how many times and how melodramatically such scenes of fidelity are presented to us, we applaud and cheer. "*Yes, that,*" we say, "There can be nothing more precious, more important, more life-saving than *that.*"

Our first reading today offers just such a scene. The Israelite prophet Elijah must make what he knows to be his last, long, lonely walk. He is dying, his enemies abound, and he prepares to leave his enemies abound, and he prepares to leave his disciple Elisha and retrace the steps of Joshua centuries before until he has crossed back over the Jordan to where Moses himself died. "Stay here, Elisha," the prophet says, "I have a long way to travel."

But Elisha will not stay put. Nor will he when they reach Bethel, nor when they reach Jericho, nor after that at the Jordan River. In the verses left out by our lectionary today, the other prophets who tag along warn or taunt Elisha (we can't be sure which), saying, "Don't you know that today the Lord will take your master away from you?"

Elisha's response to them is, "Yes, I know; keep silent." In other words, he follows Elijah with eyes wide open. And to his dying friend he says, "As the Lord lives, and as you yourself live, I will not leave you."

That gives me goose bumps. It makes my heart swell, like a scene from a good movie. I want that friend. I want walking alongside me the one will not leave me in my weakness and in my fear. But if we read this passage with care-and if we look at it alongside our Gospel reading from Luke-we see that the emphasis today is not *having* such a stalwart friend, but *being* one. And we also see why it is that such friends are so few. To *be* a friend in the darkness is a heavy load.

We know that, don't we? We've all had people in our lives who experienced grief or loss, who spiraled into loneliness and maybe even despair. Beside some we have remained. Others we walked with for a while, but over time the way became too thorny and the burden became too much. Eventually, we stayed behind. We were not faithful and true, as Elisha was to Elijah.

To make things more complicated, there are instances in which being faithful to a friend even requires allowing that friend to walk alone. If the one we love is on a willfully destructive path and will not turn around, running headlong and purposely *into* the darkness, calling the bad good, then withdrawing support that enables destructive behavior can be, paradoxically, the faithful and loving thing. In that case we walk alongside the one we love through prayer alone, and as anyone faced with such an excruciating circumstance will tell you, being that kind of friend is the hardest thing in the world to be. Sometimes we can't do it, so we do the easier thing: We continue to enable, even though we know doing so won't pull our friend from the darkness.

In Second Kings, Elijah's long walk reveals yet another aspect of fidelity: Walking the way with Elijah also means Elisha must be willing to take up his friend's mantle. Literally, when Elijah is lifted by the chariot of fire to heaven, his mantle falls at Elisha's feet. Figuratively, Elisha's fidelity to his teacher includes taking up the mantle of Elijah's cause, his very life and work. That which Elijah cherished, Elisha will now cherish. That which animated Elijah will now animate Elisha.

The first indication we see of this in the story is Elisha parting the waters of the Jordan, but his fidelity to his friend after Elijah's death is much weightier than that. Elijah spent his life speaking truth to powerful people who preferred to hear flattery. He was pitted against false prophets who wished him harm. He slept in caves with no material comfort. Being his true friend means that Elisha must be prepared for all of these things, too.

In the end, it is all these aspects of friendship, holy and true, that characterize a synonymous vocation: that of discipleship. What it means to be a disciple of Jesus is just that: to be one who walks with those who are in darkness, even when doing so requires the hard love of letting one go. It means taking on the mantle of fidelity that Jesus himself wore: a mantle of unstinting love that speaks truth and not flattery, a mantle that courageously faces a world which tells us at every turn that love is weak, a mantle that embraces friendship as infinitely more important than material things.

Nothing can substitute for this kind of friendship, for this kind of discipleship. That is why in Luke's Gospel Jesus is so adamant toward those who would half-heartedly follow him. Along his way, people approach and say, "Let me come with you, but first let me plow my field, or say goodbye, or bury the dead."

Jesus replies that it cannot be so. One must follow or not. There can be no half measures. In the Garden of Gethsemane, Jesus himself will experience what it is like to be bereft of true friends. He will sweat blood in his despair. He will know the darkness, and his demand upon those who would follow him is that we must not leave one another alone. We must be a people who remain faithful to each other.

Near the end of the Lord of the Rings saga the hobbit Frodo, so small and weak in the face of evil, collapses at the foot of the mountain where he must carry out his task. His fellow hobbit Sam tries to encourage him. Sam says it's springtime back home. Flowers are in bloom. Strawberries have ripened. "I can't recall the taste of food, Sam" Frodo replies, "I can't recall the feel of grass. I am naked in the darkness."

For a moment Sam looks ready to give up, but then from somewhere deep inside a resolve emerges. He hoists Frodo onto his shoulders and starts, with shaking knees, up the mountain. "I can't carry your burden for you, Mr. Frodo," he says, "but I can carry *you*."

How can we do it? We can, because Jesus is faithful to us. When humanity hung by a precipice, rather than flee the Garden Jesus was willing to hang on the cross. On a hill outside of Jerusalem, Jesus stayed with us to the end, and he does so yet today. There is no darkness into which he will not go. There is no path down which he will not walk with us. He is Han Solo to Luke; He is Sam to Frodo; He is Elisha to Elijah.

Because he walks with us, we can have the courage to walk with one another. And then our hearts will swell and our spirits soar, because we have remained faithful, and none of us need be alone.

Amen.

Whiplash

What just happened? Let's go back over the day. We awoke, looked outside, and thanked God for this beautiful spring. We showered and dressed, and at some point it occurred to us that today is Palm Sunday. We began humming "All glory, laud, and honor" as we drove to church. We explained to our kids—or reminded ourselves—about the palm fronds and how we'd waved them in our own childhood. And then we arrived here, ready to celebrate. "Hosanna!" was sung, with smiles and good cheer all around.

Fifteen minutes in, though, everything changed and jarringly so. Like someone crashing from a manic high into the throes of depression, our worship moved from palms to Golgotha. We've moved from joy to stunned disappointment: in the disciples, in the crowd, and—perhaps, if we're honest—in Jesus. That bit with the palms and the donkey, it seems, was all a charade.

There is a nascent movement in the Episcopal Church away from combining Palm and Passion Sundays. One of my clergy friends in Texas tells me his parish foregoes the Passion reading on this day altogether. The whiplash is too much. Let the party be the party, the celebration the celebration. And yet, the liturgical whiplash we experience on this combined day reflects accurately the speed at which the crowd in the Gospel changes its mind about Jesus.

On Palm Sunday in Matthew's Gospel, Jesus arrives at the gate of Jerusalem hot on the heels of all the news the crowd has heard about him: the healings, the miracles, the ability to generate hope and to rally a crowd. Word has preceded Jesus' coming. The people meet him as he arrives and extend the kind of hospitality reserved for dignitaries, nobility and kings: They cover the road before him with their coats and palm branches. The citizens of Jerusalem ask, "Who is he?" but for the disciples and the crowd who line the road the question is rhetorical. They've shown through their actions who they assume Jesus to be.

But Jesus' very next act upends their assumptions. He gets off that donkey and marches into the Jewish temple, and without so much as a warning he causes a riot and disrupts the market. (I guarantee you neither the crowd nor the disciples were expecting that.) Jesus angrily condemns the casual, everyday practices—the comforts—by which the people live their lives. And that's just the beginning. Then Jesus starts to tell cryptic parables of judgment, to pick fights with the academic Pharisees and the privileged and affluent Sadducees, to openly choose sides with the least, the lonely and the lost. You think we had whiplash this morning? For those who'd lined the roads to greet Jesus, he's suddenly selling them a bill of goods different from what they'd expected. The easy celebration has given way to a hard, life-shattering call to discipleship. Jesus is now demanding nothing less than death to the old life and resurrection to something entirely new.

Have you ever felt duped? Have you ever voted for a political candidate who changed his stripes as soon as he was in office? Have you ever told a trusted friend a secret only to have it come back to you third-hand? Have you ever gone into business with a colleague only to discover that he's making side deals behind your back, selling you out?

How did you respond? It's easy to move from adulation and good cheer to vicious condemnation in such circumstances. The change in our emotional state can happen in an instant and feel like whiplash. When we feel we've been taken advantage of, led along under false pretenses, made to look a fool, we seethe with resentment. We boil with anger. And we sometimes lash out. That is how this crowd can move so quickly from "Hosanna!" to "Crucify him!"

But think again to those instances when you felt duped. Put on a fresh, clear set of lenses. Sometimes, to be sure, we are betrayed. But other times, our resentment comes not because the other person has wronged us, but because he has with steely honesty and hard love pointed out our wrong. Sometimes our anger is the consequence of being called to the carpet for our own rationalizations, our own misdeeds, our own subtly destructive ways of living. Sometimes the one standing before us presents us with the way of rebirth to new life that requires first giving up the old life. And we lash out against the bearer of truth because we do not want to hear, to see, the truth. If we silence the messenger we can continue to pretend that the falseness of our lives is the truth.

That is, friends, what Palm Sunday: the Sunday of the Passion is all about. The question posed to the crowd is not rhetorical after all: "Who is he?"

Who is Jesus for us? Is he the easy, non-political, feel-good dazzler? Is he the one who heals and hugs us without question and without challenge? If that is the Jesus we worship, if that's one we're willing to call "Lord," then we'd better skip Holy Week and go straight to Easter with its pastel eggs and white shoes.

Because the Jesus who steps off that donkey is the bearer of God's truth about what kills and what gives life. Jesus' words are harsh. His upending truth about what we prioritize in our lives and to what life-diminishing things we give value is startling. Love, you see, is hard as iron when it seeks to save someone walking in darkness. Jesus loves us too much to be silent, and he will not compromise the hard words of love we need to hear. The people of his own day were no more willing to hear the truth than we are, and as a result Jesus' path of love for us, as we'll see this week if we have the courage to participate and experience it with him, unavoidably leads to the Cross.

That's where we're invited to go with him, not to be crucified—blessedly, he does that on our behalf—but to stand at the foot of the Cross. We are not to melt away from the truth like the disciples, to deny that we know the truth like Peter, or to lash out against the truth like the crowd. We are to witness in faith what is happening there on the Cross, what new life is being made available to us that renders all the cheap dazzle we've previously known worthless. We are to answer the question "Who is he?" with the Centurion who stays when all others flee and cries to the heavens, "Truly, this man was God's son!"

Amen.

Following the Outlaw Jesus

JANUARY 2012   MARK 1:14-20

Now after John the Baptist was arrested, Jesus came to Galilee, proclaiming the good news of God, and saying, 'The time is fulfilled, and the kingdom of God has come near; repent, and believe in the good news.'

As Jesus passed along the Sea of Galilee, he saw Simon and his brother Andrew casting a net into the lake—for they were fishermen. And Jesus said to them, 'Follow me and I will make you fish for people.' And immediately they left their nets and followed him. As he went a little farther, he saw James son of Zebedee and his brother John, who were in their boat mending the nets. Immediately he called them; and they left their father Zebedee in the boat with the hired men, and followed him.

Ninety-nine percent of all motorcycle gangs are law-abiding. That's comforting, I suppose, except for what it implies about the other one percent! Indeed, there are motorcycle gangs who refer to themselves as "one-percenters," which means they take pride in their status as the one percent of bikers who are also outlaws. The most well-known one-percenter gang is the Hell's Angels. Others, who are less notorious, but no more law-abiding, are the Pagans and the Bandidos. One-percenters distrust and subvert the authorities. They exist just outside acceptable society.

In Mark's Gospel, we read about another group that travels the road together. Today, the first four recruits are enlisted, but eventually there will be twelve members plus their leader, enough to qualify as a gang. They, too, distrust and subvert authority. They, too, find themselves just outside the bounds of what society considers acceptable. And their leader? He was trained and formed by an outlaw—John the Baptist—as today's Gospel reveals in a throwaway line at the outset, "Now after John was arrested, Jesus came to Galilee..." In fact, this gang's leader will eventually find himself executed as an outlaw between two outlaws.

I became fascinated by outlaw motorcycle gangs—one-percenters—a few months ago when I found on Facebook an old high school friend, Todd, with whom I'd lost contact. Todd's Facebook profile included a graphic with fluorescent green lettering and a cartoon red devil. The graphic read "Brazos," and I was intrigued enough to do a quick Google search. It turns out "Brazos" refers to the Brazos Motorcycle Club, a one-percenter outlaw gang, and I soon learned that my friend is a Brazos "prospect," or probationary member.[1]

Depending on which news outlet one reads, the Brazos Motorcycle Club runs guns, traffics in drugs, and otherwise participates in organized crime. I don't know how much of that is true, but I do know the *Huffington Post* reports that recently the Los Angeles Brazos got into a gunfight with a rival Hell's Angels chapter over which gang could lay claim to the neighborhood Starbucks. (Only in the twenty-first century, I suppose!) Two men ended up dead from gunshot wounds.[2]

Not wanting to learn nitty-gritty details that might require him to kill me, I did not ask Todd any questions about Brazos, but I did begin to frequent his Facebook profile and monitor what he was doing.

Soon, virtually every post on Todd's profile referenced the motorcycle gang. Todd even changed his name to "Knuckles Slide," a moniker apparently given him by the club. He was marked, by tattooing his entire right arm in a virtual sleeve of flames. He now wears only green, including a denim vest covered in Brazos patches. Todd—a fire fighter by training—has even given up his job and opened a new small business with its own logo printed in that conspicuous Brazos fluorescent green. I suspect the business is a front for the motorcycle gang. One day another Brazos prospect posted on Todd's wall about how arduous the membership process for the gang is. Todd's response was, "It takes everything you've got, but it's worth it."

The call of Simon and Andrew, James and John to follow Jesus is actually not so different. Jesus walks by and says, "Follow me," from which a number of radical moves occur. These four are the middle class of their day. They own their own boats and nets. They provide for their families. And yet, something about Jesus causes them to leave it all behind. They give up their livelihood and front for a leader who will refuse again and again to concede to societal convention. Simon will even receive a new name—Peter, the Rock—indicative of an entirely new identity. These four and their friends will be faced repeatedly, both before and after the death of their leader, with situations that demand they either present the easy way the world deems acceptable or else in their words and actions— with every decision, large and small—present an alternative way of being, one that declares God's grace at work in their lives as evidently as if they were covered in fluorescent green patches.

That's what it means, after all, to "fish for people." It means for the followers of Jesus to participate in his work evidently, overtly, and contrary to what people expect and accept. These four who Jesus calls today will, essentially, give up who they are when they become members of Jesus' gang. Except we don't call them members. We have a special name for this kind of loyalty, this kind of self-giving. We call it discipleship.

On his Facebook page, my friend Todd lists his religion as "agnostic," but it isn't so. Everything about Todd makes clear that his religion is, in fact, the Brazos Motorcycle Club. He has laid his life at its feet. He has changed his name and marked his body and given away everything for its cause. Todd has become a disciple of the Brazos gang, and that is, by any definition, a religious commitment.

I find myself asking: What is it that makes someone give up everything for identity in a one-percenter gang engaged in brutal criminal activity? Likely, part of the allure is power, a sense of invincibility that comes with traveling the road among others who carry guns and move about in a pack. But I suspect a bigger part is that the Brazos care for Todd. In a world in which purpose is superficial and fleeting, they give him meaning. And, he has become an icon for them, via his name, his attire, the markings on his very body, and his daily labor. As Todd said, "It takes everything you've got, but it's worth it."

Now, a harder question for us: If Todd can turn his life over, wholly and willingly, to a one-percenter motorcycle gang, to a group of thugs who stage shootouts at Starbucks, why can't we turn our lives over to Jesus the Christ, who bleeds grace and saves us?

When one meets Todd—excuse me, Knuckles Slide—on the street, there is no doubt that he is a Brazos disciple. When one meets us, is there any indication at all in our names, in our dress, in our words and our actions that we have given our lives away, that we are disciples of that outlaw crucified between two outlaws?

Todd is marked by a right arm tattooed in a sleeve of flame. Lest we forget, *we, too, are marked*, sealed on our foreheads by the Holy Spirit in baptism and marked as Christ's own forever. We are not members of this or any church, not primarily. We are disciples of the outlaw Jesus, who declares pardon where the world would condemn, who loves where the world would hate, who extends grace where the world would sow suffering.

There is power in following this Jesus. There is strength. For those who live in Christ, ultimately and forever we are invincible. But more importantly, Jesus the Christ cares for us—loves us—and when we gather around him and with one another, we are able to embody that care in ways that can move the world from brokenness to grace. We disciples can become icons of the outlaw Jesus we claim to serve. And when we do, our lives take on meaning unlike anything we've ever experienced, a meaning so deep that all worldly locations of meaning—including the Brazos Motorcycle Club—look like grotesque caricatures by comparison.

Jesus calls us today. "The time is fulfilled," he says. "The kingdom of God is near." When you leave this place, will anyone know you are a member of this outlaw gang? Will anyone see the mark? Will your words, your actions and your decisions reveal the leader in whom you find deepest meaning, your very life, and your new name, Christian? It takes everything we've got to follow the outlaw Jesus, but it's worth it.

Amen.

ENDNOTES

1 I have changed the names both of my friend and of the motorcycle gang.

2 Anna Almendrala, "Hells Angels Gang Fight With Vagos Motorcycle Club Results In 2 Dead, Several Wounded," *The Huffington Post*, 27 October, 2011, http://www.huffingtonpost.com/2011/10/27/hells-angels-gang-fight-w_n_1062730.html.

Word

Immersed in the Word

DECEMBER 2011   JOHN 1:1-13

In the beginning was the Word, and the Word was with God, and the Word was God... He was in the beginning with God. All things came into being through him, and without him not one thing came into being. What has come into being in him was life, and the life was the light of all people. The light shines in the darkness, and the darkness did not overcome it. There was a man sent from God, whose name was John. He came as a witness to testify to the light, so that all might believe through him. He himself was not the light, but he came to testify to the light. The true light, which enlightens everyone, was coming into the world. He was in the world, and the world came into being through him; yet the world did not know him. He came to what was his own, and his own people did not accept him. But to all who received him, who believed in his name, he gave power to become children of God, who were born, not of blood or of the will of the flesh or of the will of man, but of God.

Thank you for inviting me to be with you this morning.[1] This place is lovely, the church is beautiful, and your hospitality is gracious. I've studied the list of preachers who have stood before you prior to my coming, and it's more than a little daunting. Even so, I am glad to be here. Connecticut is foreign to me.

When I imagine a map of the United States in my mind's eye, it appears like those maps of magic kingdoms and fantasy lands in children's books. Just north of the Mason-Dixon Line, everything drops off into hazy mist. That said, I have a clergy friend from Massachusetts, and he assures me that I have nothing to fear venturing so far from the Shire.

I did my undergraduate work at Hendrix College, a nationally-ranked liberal arts school in central Arkansas, very like Hamilton College in upstate New York or Bowdoin College in Maine. For two years after graduation, I was privileged to work in the admission office at Hendrix, and my particular area of responsibility was coordinating the campus visitation program for high school students and their parents. The Dean was John Churchill, a Yale PhD and a Rhodes Scholar, who now serves as the Executive Director of *Phi Beta Kappa* in Washington.

Now, neither Dean Churchill nor I was born into august circumstances. John is from tiny Hector, Arkansas, and I was born in Paragould, a Northeast Arkansas delta town known for its quirks. I was raised hiking up and down Eight Mile Creek, visiting friends whose spacious homes were actually double-wide trailers, and passing through nearby towns with names like Possum Grape, Toad Suck, and—this is true—Goobertown. My father is an attorney and a very good one, but Andy Griffith's Mayberry may be a better depiction of my hometown than Harper Lee's *To Kill a Mockingbird*.

All that is to say, Hendrix College was Eden to me. There, I was immersed in words. I relished my exposure to philosophy and the arts, and over time the patterns of my speech modulated and the topics of my conversation expanded.

And so, one fine Arkansas spring day in 1996 I stood as a Hendrix College admissions counselor before the assembled banquet hall of visiting prospective families to ask whether everyone had finished a delicious meal and was ready for the campus tour. I stood in navy blue suit and crisp Oxford shirt, with my hair parted neatly and my tie on straight.

My mouth opened, but instead of eloquence I uttered, to my own surprise really, "Y'all done eatin' yet?"

Dean Churchill took the microphone from me and without missing a beat said, "You can take the boy out of Paragould but you can't take Paragould out of the boy!"

"In the beginning was the Word...All things came into being through him, and without him not one thing came into being. What has come into being in him is life...to all who receive him, who believe in his name, he gives power to become children of God..."

In 1879, a Scottish teacher named James Murray launched the largest lexicographical project in human history. It was as audacious as it was bold: Murray, with the backing of the Oxford University Press, would compile a dictionary that included every single word in the English language, along with a definitive history of each word's usage, sometimes going back centuries. The end result would be the *Oxford English Dictionary* or *OED*.[2] Ultimately, it would span twelve volumes and require forty years to complete.

At the same time Professor Murray was coming of age in Scotland, a different man, an American army surgeon named William Minor, was slipping into madness. Minor had seen horror at the Battle of the Wilderness in the Civil War, and he had been forced by his superiors to brand a fellow soldier on the cheek with a hot iron "D" for the man's attempt to desert. These experiences unhinged him. After spending a year and a half in a military asylum, Minor was allowed to resign his commission and retire.

For reasons unknown, Dr. Minor then moved across the ocean to the slums of South London, and there, late one night, he aimed and fired a pistol at a man (who was on his way home from work to his wife and six children), killing him. In his delusion, Dr. Minor believed the man was about to attack him.

Dr. Minor was committed to an asylum an hour south of London where he devolved further into madness, until one day he read in a magazine a plea from Professor James Murray for educated men to assist with the compiling of the proposed *Oxford English Dictionary*. The one thing to which William Minor had free access in the asylum was books, and with some faint glimmer of lucidity—call it prevenient grace—he plunged himself into the work. He immersed himself in words.

When he did, an amazing thing happened. Somehow, the words served as a life preserver. They pulled him up from the abyss of madness, and William Minor became the single largest contributor to the *OED*. He began a correspondence with Professor Murray that carried on for years. His definitions and quotations were lyrical, his research profound. Dr. Minor found life in the words, and when Professor Murray finally traveled to meet him in person, years after they'd met via the Queen's post, Murray was shocked to discover Dr. Minor's dark past. The William Minor with whom he had corresponded for years was not a product of madness, but of light and life.

"In the beginning was the Word…All things came into being through him, and without him not one thing came into being. What has come into being in him is life…to all who receive him, who believe in his name, he gives power to become children of God…"

Mary Adelzadeh is a land conversation specialist for the Stewardship Council in the American Southwest. Mary works diligently to ensure that land usage in that arid region is sustainable. She also works with Native American youth to promote their culture and sense of self-worth. Mary is a remarkable woman who I was privileged to meet and know at an Aspen Institute seminar last October. But statistically and sociologically, she shouldn't have been there.

Mary's mother is Navajo, and her father is Persian. He fled Iran when the Shah fell. The parents' marriage didn't last, and Mary's family cycled into a familiar poverty. Her mother scraped together a living by cleaning houses. There was no money for childcare, and, desperate for somewhere safe to lodge her kids during the long work day, Mary's mother would drop them off each morning at the rural public library where they would spend hours wandering the stacks, immersed in the words.

Mary told me she "formed a relationship with the books, with the words." And that relationship made all the difference. Worlds that would have remained closed miraculously opened. What might have been dead-end darkness in her life gave way to light, and Mary discovered dimensions of life and possibility, all because of the words.

What has all this to do with us, we who are gathered here early on a chilly Friday morning for coffee and breakfast? This is no lexicography study. It is a preaching event. But one more story first:

After years spent in stifling boarding schools, C.S. Lewis tells of coming under the tutelage of a beloved old teacher he calls "The Great Knock." The Great Knock insisted that young Jack Lewis learn Greek. He was required to read Greek, translate Greek, and even speak Greek. In another language, he was immersed in the words. At first the exercise was laborious and boring, but eventually, Lewis says, "I became able to understand a great deal without (even mentally) translating it; I was beginning to think in Greek. That is the great Rubicon to cross in learning any language. Those in whom the Greek word lives only while they are hunting for it in the lexicon, and who then substitute the English word for it, are not reading the Greek at all; they are only solving a puzzle."[3]

Lewis had truly learned a new language when he began to think in it. And note how he describes this: In him, he says, the word lived.

And *that* is what these tales have to do with us and our faith. You see, our faith is not an undifferentiated acknowledgement of some mystical divinity. Our faith is not primarily a moral code that will keep us virtuous and our communities clean. Our faith is not merely a longing for the joys of heaven in the great hereafter.

Our faith is in a living Word and a Word that lives in us, the Word—the Christ— through whom all things are made.

> *"In the beginning was the Word...All things came into being through him, and without him not one thing came into being. What has come into being in him is life...to all who receive him, who believe in his name, he gives power to become children of God..."*

Too often, our approach to faith is like the study habits of the student who only superficially learns a new language. We approach life as a series of puzzles to be solved and religion as the dictionary or guidebook. When we want a quick, good answer to make sense of a chaotic world, we consult the resources of faith. At all other times, we leave that faith safely put away, like a book on the shelf.

And that, friends, is an exercise that will always fail to satisfy. Faith is not a dictionary to solve life's puzzles. Borrowing C.S. Lewis' phrase, faith is a Rubicon to cross. Faith is a new language to be learned so fully and intimately that we think and dream in it. Faith is immersion in the Word.

C.S. Lewis believed the world to be full of signposts that point us toward the truth of our faith, and the stories with which I began do that very thing. For William Minor, the terror of the world left him grasping at sanity by his fingertips. And yet, when he focused the whole of his being on learning and serving words, light broke through his darkness.

For us, too, when we commit the all of us to knowing and serving the Word, we find ourselves lifted up and pulled free from the madness that licks from the darkness around us.

For Mary Adelzadeh, the world's circumstances conspired to render her a victim of the cycle of poverty. The world determined to consign her to a script already written. But Mary, by her own account, "formed a relationship with words" as she walked the library stacks day after day, and that relationship made the impossible, possible. She threw away the world's script for her and instead walked down the newly lighted path.

For us, too, a relationship with the Word, in which we spend our days steeped in its presence, creates new possibilities for who we can be and what we can do in the world. Light shines on new paths where once there was only shadow.

What I'm saying is, of course, about Holy Scripture, about studying and knowing the Word as incarnate in the words of the Bible. But please don't mistake that it is all, or even primarily, about that. The words of Holy Scripture are but windows to the Word, Jesus the Christ through whom we and this world are made, who seeks to be in relationship with us, whose desire it is that we know him as he knows us.

That kind of relationship, that kind of knowledge, that kind of language only come when we are immersed in the Word Jesus Christ. Our waking must be in conversation with the Word; our eyes must be attuned to see the Word incarnate in those we meet; our cries must be to the Word who shines light in the darkness; and our rest must be in anticipation that the Word will be in our slumbering dreams.

When we receive Christ in this way, when he sinks into the marrow of us and meets the Word already incarnate there, then through his power we indeed become children of God, finding health and sanity in a maddened world and knowing the new language so well that it becomes our primary one.

The Rubicon awaits. The only question is whether we'll cross it.

Amen.

ENDNOTES

1 This sermon was delivered at the "Men on Fire" preaching series at Christ Episcopal Church, Greenwich, Connecticut.

2 See Simon Winchester, *The Professor and the Madman* (New York: HarperCollins, 1998). The subsequent story about James Murray and William Minor is drawn from Winchester's text.

3 C. S. Lewis, *Surprised by Joy* (Orlando, FL: Harcourt, 1955), 141.

About the Author

The Very Reverend Barkley Thompson is Dean of Christ Church Cathedral (Episcopal) in Houston Texas. He has also served parishes in Collierville, Tennessee (a suburb of Memphis) and Roanoke, Virginia. Barkley holds degrees from Hendrix College, The University of Chicago, and the Seminary of the Southwest in Austin, Texas.

.

Made in the USA
Charleston, SC
22 December 2013